# HENRY JAMES:
# Fiction as History

# HENRY JAMES:
## Fiction as History

edited by
## Ian F. A. Bell

VISION
and
BARNES & NOBLE

Vision Press Limited
Fulham Wharf
Townmead Road
London SW6 2SB

and

Barnes & Noble Books
81 Adams Drive
Totowa, NJ 07512

ISBN (UK) 0 85478 016 5
ISBN (US) 0 389 20515 X

Printed and bound in Great Britain by
Unwin Brothers Ltd.,
Old Woking, Surrey.
Phototypeset by Galleon Photosetting,
Ipswich, Suffolk.
MCMLXXXIV

# Contents

# Introduction

Tzvetan Todorov, in an essay of 1969, made an important complaint about the way in which James has generally been read: 'James has been ranked among the authors inaccessible to the common reader, and only professionals are "qualified" to appreciate his overcomplicated art.'[1] It is not to the first half of Todorov's complaint that the present collection wishes to address itself, the myth of the 'common reader', but to the latter half, those 'professionals' in the academies whose appreciation of James's fiction justifies itself in large part by valorizing this very over-complication. In this context, James may be seen as sharing the larger features exhibited by classic modernist writing in general, that of Pound, Eliot and Joyce, principally the great problem of closure: or, in other words, the possibilities for intervention and for imagining alternative worlds on the part of the reader. Such closure is perpetuated by the kind of 'professional' critical practice that gives rise to Todorov's unease, practice which, by its emphasis in particular upon James's own insistence on 'technique' and presentation, has effectively appropriated these terms as items within its own privileged discourse. This effect in turn consolidates a proposal for an intangible, highly sophisticated web of rarefied consciousness which indeed requires equally polished and trained skills to unravel.

The present volume inserts itself as a request for a more genuinely democratic system of reading which will be more true to the Jamesian *oeuvre* in its own right and will liberate readers from the abstractive prison of a precious and wrongly sensitized rhetoric. The formalism which James's fiction undoubtedly invites, requires, quite simply, readings which attempt to re-structure it out of pure aesthetics in order to recognize the ruptures and difficulties of its historical occasions.

7

John Goode, in introducing what has been undoubtedly the best collection of essays on James published during the last decade, has commented: 'James has been less worshipped than processed; the endless exegeses are little manufactures.'[2] In a sense, we are now in a position to reverse these terms; it is precisely the failure of Jamesian commentaries to recognize the relationship between their own 'process' as a 'manufacture' and the objects of their interest that perpetuates the notion of a sealed, privileged world which has so little cognisance of itself as a structure whose activity can only properly be understood as manufactured. Such a world refuses to admit its own history of being made and the concomitant arena of its own social relationships.

Paradoxically, what critics from both ends of the political spectrum have agreed upon is the proposed negativity of James's own politics. For both, the spectre of James's concern with his own art precludes any interest in a novelistic reliance upon social density by which we customarily measure a writer's alertness to the seemingly 'real' issues of the conditions from which his compositions emerge. But James's endless interrogations into his own practice, his analysis of the production of literary effects, from the early essays on Balzac and the study of Hawthorne through to the Prefaces for the New York edition of the novels, exhibit exactly the opposite of such supposed negativity. Here, surely, we witness one of the most sustained displays in modernist writing of its own manufacture; we see how the trick of fiction is performed, we are offered the grounds for our own intervention. To argue that James's display is merely a sophisticated version of art for art's sake and then to claim this as politically innocent is to misunderstand the whole Jamesian enterprise and to abuse the equipment we have for dealing with it. The present collection has no intention to authorize a form of uniformity in approaching James, nor has the editorial position any wish to speak on behalf of its contributors, but both may assume as an epigraph some propositions from Leo Bersani who has attended brilliantly to this question of James's politics.

Bersani begins with the assumption that James is interested in the types of discourse produced by the exercise of power. Although James ignores power 'as the presumed possession of

8

those who govern', he composes a dialogue which is 'almost an abstract diagram' of political process:

> That is, it maps out the intimidations and negotiated concessions which come into play as a result of the imbalances and inequalities immediately produced by a relation between two 'points' (two human subjects). In composing dialogue, the intensely political novelist is primarily interested neither in using talk as a means of moving his story ahead nor in allowing his characters to make a scenic display of the essential psychic drives behind their behaviour. Rather, like James, he organises talk in view of multiple local effects to redress the balance of power, to apply the always unstable pressures and counter-pressures which repeatedly and briefly subject the other to the speaker's control.[3]

Bersani's analysis implicitly relies on utterance as the key to meaning, rather as Volosinov insisted on the dialogical nature of any true epistemology which creates the space where meaning is socially generated and where intervention is thereby enabled.[4] In purely Jamesian terms, this becomes a concern with talk at the expense of action, with the 'geometry' of relations. For Bersani, the politics of James's fiction become visible in the equivalence established by his characters between the exercise of power and knowledge:

> Pressures are applied, gains are made, retreats are covered almost entirely through a complex system which manufactures things to be known. The awe with which a Jamesian hero announces that he 'sees,' or that someone else 'knows,' expresses his thrilled appreciation of the extended field of power created by each new luminous insight. And *not* to know what someone else knows is a correlative loss of power.

More importantly, it is on the basis of this equivalence between power and the knowledge produced or concealed dialogically that Bersani is able to relate the distinctive and awkward mimesis of James's work to the function of literature in its wider sphere. It is James's efforts to deconstruct the novelistic pretensions of fiction that permit his work its proper access to the 'real' beyond the confinements of the rhetoric of realism:

> Because of James's remarkable indifference to that diversification of behaviour by which other novelists seek to convince us

9

that their characters have more than verbal authority, his novels demystify literature's claim to be a reflector of nonliterary life and they diagram the specific mechanisms of power when its exercise is limited to verbal exchanges.[5]

These literary diagrams, by virtue of their very removal from novelistic furniture, thus have 'the exemplary value of demonstrating that transactions of power always involve communications, and that these communications frequently take the form of equivocal donations of knowledge'. Here, then, lies the core of James's political function: 'literature, exactly because it is power enacted uniquely as a form of organized knowledge, can serve the politically useful rôle of dramatizing the nothingness of all epistemological fictions.'[6]

The following essays instigate a variety of means for reading out of James's formalism more productive schemata than, hitherto, have been available for identifying its social and historical provenance. Their ambition is to re-constitute the conditions exposed by James's efforts to re-compose the nature of fiction and thereby to politicize those determinants of fiction which, notoriously, have been understood by liberal aesthetics as resistant to issues expressible beyond the arena of art.

I.F.A.B.

University of Keele

## NOTES

1. Tzvetan Todorov, 'The Secret of Narrative' in *The Poetics of Prose*, trans. Richard Howard (Oxford, 1977), p. 143.
2. *The Air of Reality*, ed. John Goode (London, 1972), p. 1.
3. Leo Bersani, 'The Subject of Power', *Diacritics* (Fall, 1977), 10.
4. V. N. Volosinov, *Marxism and the Philosophy of Language* (1930), trans. Ladislav Matejka and I. R. Titunik (New York and London, 1973), p. 105.
5. Bersani, loc. cit., p. 10.
6. Ibid., pp. 10–11, 12.

# 1

# Money, History and Writing in Henry James: Assaying *Washington Square*

by IAN F. A. BELL

*1*

James's project in *Washington Square*, as I have suggested elsewhere,[1] marks an interest in certain forms of abstraction and human paralysis detectable in the onset of corporate industry in America during the 1830s and 1840s. His concern takes shape in the very structure of the novel, its extraordinary specificity concerning time and place in the opening three chapters which is progressively dissolved as the action of the story begins from chapter four onwards. The Square itself, conceived as an 'ideal of quiet and genteel retirement'[2] against the commercial turbulence of lower Manhattan, loses its relational context within the city and inhabits a kind of timelessness. Both of these are defining features of the industrial production of commodities. They are equally features of the bourgeois temperament that James is concerned to diagnose in the balanced, rational discourse of Dr. Sloper and the vacuous jangle of Mrs. Penniman's impoverished imagination.[3] It is these styles, in company with the problematically 'natural' style of the socially indefinable Townsend, which compete for the commodified Catherine, worth 'eighty thousand a year' (pp. 27 and 29), within the frozen world of market practice. Their

11

competition, at a specific moment in American economic history, enables us to read an intimate relationship between forms of writing, forms of history and forms of financial behaviour, a relationship which may be focused through one of the main questions presented by the novel: what informs James's choice of this earlier period in American history as the location for a work written during the late 1870s?

Millicent Bell has written well of the problem of 'model' for James during the time of *Washington Square*, particularly that of the minutely itemized realism offered by the Novel of Balzac. The period 1878–79 seems, she rightly notes, 'to have been pivotal in James's career, a time when Balzac's and all other models both teased and repelled'. She illuminatingly suggests that it was, in part, a recognition of Balzac's inappropriateness which forged the perimeters of James's own procedures, 'the use of central consciousness whose confinement of scope was its interest'.[4] More immediately, of course, there was the question of the Romance and Hawthorne whose rôle as resource was equally as testing and ambivalent.[5] To schematize broadly, we might suggest that the interference of Novelistic and Romantic worlds, codified by Balzac and Hawthorne respectively, may prove useful in considering the relationship between writing and the social forms of commerce which constitutes the strategy of *Washington Square*.

One of the main complications of the novel is Catherine's quietude. Her rare-spokenness and broken syntax articulate both the object of James's disquiet (by its paralysed, non-dialogical incapacity) and the putative alternative to it (as an increasingly impossible gesture towards authenticity and a freedom from lexical and institutional impositions).[6] It is thus simultaneously frozen in the material world that we experience (as a reminder of the unchangeability of commodities, their denial of their own production) and a resistance against such materiality (as a Romantic refusal of discourse to taint itself by a world already given). James's sympathy is powerfully invested in both the inhumanity of the former and the possibilities of the latter, and the simultaneity of their occasion marks a point at which he may exploit the extent to which his own discourse belongs to the ideological equipment of its opposition. In other words, the situation of Catherine may be read as an index to James's negotiation of Balzac and Hawthorne, and his interest in the urge, encouraged by novelistic convention, to locate the alternative worlds of fiction within the world we ordinarily experience.[7] His elisions of time and space (the two indispensable properties of that convention) are, again, features of the bourgeois temperament he analyses. For such a temperament, as Alfred Sohn-Rethel notes, 'time becomes unhistorical time and space ungeographical space' in order to assume a 'character of absolute historical timelessness and universality'.[8] Time, indeed, is not only elided in *Washington Square* but operates as a distinct temporal confusion whereby, despite its overwhelming 'realistic' specificity, its chronology competes within itself for historical place and emerges as an explicitly unstable resource for finding one's bearings.[9] It is not insignificant that James also disrupts a third novelistic property at the very end of the first chapter; this is the voice which authorizes our reception of the narrative, and it is disrupted in a way which confuses and disguises authorial utterance to finish with a recognizably Hawthornesque mysteriousness about its entire enterprise:

> [Catherine] grew up a very robust and healthy child, and her father, as he looked at her, often *said to himself* that, such as she was, he at least need have no fear of losing her. *I say* 'such as she was,' because, to tell the truth—But this is a truth of which I will defer the telling. (My emphasis, p. 5)

Here, we may invoke James's famous insistence on technique, figured by a series of geometrical metaphors, which marks a clear resistance to the material world by its advocation of surface and relationship at the expense of novelistic furniture.[10] This is not to say, of course, that we are presented with a reductive model whereby we read competing fictions of the real and the imagined, but to register James's willingness to confront the risk of alienating the novel form as a social force, a willingness that may be inferred from his interest in the complex of the Novel/Romance, the material/immaterial, presented by Balzac/Hawthorne.[11] An excellent essay by Leo Bersani has attended to Jamesian geometry in order to read its distances and abstractness as more realistic than the conventional psychology of novelistic fiction:

13

It's as if he came to feel that a kind of autonomous geometric pattern, in which the parts appeal for their value to nothing but their contributive place in the essentially abstract pattern, *is* the artist's more successful representation of life. . . . The only faithful picture of life in art is not in the choice of a significant subject (James always argued against that pseudorealistic prejudice), but rather in the illustration of sense—of design-making processes. James proves the novel's connection with life by deprecating its derivation from life; and it's when he is most abstractly articulating the growth of a structure that James is also most successfully defending the mimetic function of art (and of criticism).[12]

There is much valuable suggestion in this statement. It recognizes that the pervasive Jamesian subject, freedom, is to be understood 'in the sense of inventions so coercive that they resist any attempt to enrich—or reduce—them with meaning'.[13] It suggests the principle of re-composition not only on behalf of James's own practice but also on behalf of the liberty of both his characters and his readers. James's analyses of his craft, his geometry of fictional and human behaviour, may thus be seen as a means of exhibiting his own production, enabling his fictions to display their own process, to escape the realms of mystification and to make themselves available for interventions, for re-composition, by others. By maintaining this possibility for re-composition, for imagining alternative worlds (perhaps the single most important lesson he learned from Hawthorne[14]), James refuses to appropriate the freedom of his readers. He resists the potential of his fiction to compete with a world that is solidly and confiningly familiar to us. James's predilection for the geometry of what he called 'that magnificent and masterly indirectness' enables us to see, as Todorov puts it, 'only the vision of someone and never the object of that vision directly'.[15] Liberty in style and in behaviour are thus equally guaranteed by obliquity of angle. Again, here, we recognize the tensile area that is the major theme of *Washington Square* through the risk James takes in the approximation between his own practice and the bourgeois temperament it seeks to denote. The abstractness of Jamesian design finds its uncomfortable correlative (albeit in a reductive form) in the paralysing categories of Dr. Sloper's scientism and in the sphere of exchange breached from the sphere of use to which Sloper's equalizing, non-dialogical discourse belongs.

## 2

Jamesian notions of freedom, then, are intimately bound up with styles of writing, with the imagining of alternatives. This intimacy was Hawthorne's great lesson, particularly in his Preface to *The House of the Seven Gables* where, having established his 'moral' (itself, a cry against the impositions of one generation upon another), he wishes not 'relentlessly to impale the story with its moral as an iron rod—or, rather, as by sticking a pin through a butterfly—thus at once depriving it of life, and causing it to stiffen in an ungainly and unnatural attitude'. The 'latitude' he claims for himself in the Romance rather than the Novel form is extended to the reader in warning him against that 'inflexible and exceedingly dangerous species of criticism' which attempts to bring 'his fancy pictures almost into positive contact with the realities of the moment'. The desired effect is to be a 'laying out a street that infringes upon nobody's private rights'.[16]

James appreciates the aesthetics of Hawthorne's position when he writes on behalf of this novel that 'Hawthorne was not a realist. He had a high sense of reality.' Despite the superabundance of the items which constitute 'realism' in the *Notebooks*, Hawthorne 'never attempted to render exactly or closely the actual facts of the society that surrounded him'.[17] The result, for James, is a sense of how 'reality' might be offered without the rhetoric of 'realism':

> I have said—I began by saying—that his pages were full of its spirit, and of a certain reflected light that springs from it; but I was careful to add that the reader must look for his local and national quality between the lines of his writing and in the *indirect* testimony of his tone, his accent, his temper, of his very omissions and suppressions.[18]

A little later, in considering the 'finest thing' in *The Blithedale Romance* (the character of Zenobia, 'the nearest approach that Hawthorne has made to the complete creation of a person'), James remembered Hawthorne's warning against too close an association between characters of fiction and those of experienced life; in this instance, Margaret Fuller:

> There is no strictness in the representation by novelists of persons who have struck them in life, and there can in the nature of things be none. From the moment the imagination takes a hand in the game, the inevitable tendency is to divergence, to following what may be called new scents.[19]

The complexity of James's understanding here (which inhibits any mechanistic valorization of either of the complex's defining terms over the other) may be noted by comparing the above passage with his simultaneous admiration for the presentation of the narrator in this novel, a character whose standpoint has 'the advantage of being a concrete one' and who is 'no longer, as in the preceding tales, a disembodied spirit, imprisoned in the haunted chamber of his own contemplations' but 'a particular man, with a certain human grossness'.[20] Significantly, James's final judgement on *The Blithedale Romance* employs the rhetoric of realism itself to regret that the story fails, to his sense, to avail itself of 'so excellent an opportunity for describing unhackneyed specimens of human nature' so that we 'get too much out of reality, and cease to feel beneath our feet the firm ground of an appeal to our own vision of the world, our observation'. The 'brethren of Brook Farm' may well have regretted, James suggests, that Hawthorne 'should have treated their institution mainly as a perch for starting upon an imaginative flight'.[21]

The quotations given in the preceding paragraph are, of course, all taken from the study of Hawthorne published by James immediately prior to his composition of *Washington Square* and in which he describes the America of the 1840s, the period of most of the story's action, as 'given up to a great material prosperity, a homely *bourgeois* activity' where, among the 'cultivated classes' was found

> much relish for the utterances of a writer who would help one to take a picturesque view of one's internal possibilities, and to find in the landscape of the soul all sorts of fine sunrise and moonlight effects.[22]

It is difficult to detect the extent of James's irony here, expressed as it is with a sort of warmth or, at least, of

16

understanding; but this is exactly the exercise of Mrs. Penniman's theatrical response to the bourgeois world which comfortably encloses her, with her 'natural disposition to embellish any subject that she touched' and her all-pervasive 'sense of the picturesque' (pp. 219 and 222). Her's is a drama which drastically fails the great Jamesian test of discrimination, a stage on which 'the idea of last partings occupied a place inferior in dignity only to that of first meetings' (p. 207). Mrs. Penniman's refusal of difference matches the refusal of history and materiality within the commodity relation itself as her style, like that of Sloper, reifies the world into the immutability of exchange cut off from use. We are not, of course, proposing Mrs. Penniman as a reader of Hawthorne, but noting the entanglement of James's study with his novel's temporal location and its bourgeois characteristics. As Edel notes, it was while James was working on *Washington Square* during the winter of 1879–80 that *Hawthorne* 'created its storm in the American press'.[23] And, certainly, not only James's complex of fictional strategies explored in the study but that 'storm' itself create an arena across which the novel may be read. His sense of the limits and the extent of both the Romance and the Novel points the interstitial field of the text and the insubstantiality that it risks.

One of the few concrete remarks James makes about *Washington Square* is in his famous reply to Howells' review of *Hawthorne* where he describes it as 'a tale purely American, the writing of which made me feel acutely the want of the 'paraphernalia'.[24] Here we may begin to see why James chooses to give his story an American setting rather than the English setting its 'germ' more easily suggests. The 'paraphernalia' is Howells' term for the 'items of high civilisation', Ascot, Eton, etc., James lists as absent from American life in *Hawthorne*.[25] James's reply recodes these 'items' within their more general categories which constitute a novelist's material, 'manners, customs, usages, habits, forms', and maintains their 'realist' provenance: 'I shall feel refuted only when we have produced (. . .) a gentleman who strikes me as a novelist—as belonging to the company of Balzac and Thackeray.'[26] However, in *Hawthorne* itself, James's 'items' belong to a rather more complicated sense of composition whereby the realistic and the romantic are not to be so conveniently separated. On the page preceding his list, James quotes from the Preface to *The Marble Faun*, the only novel that Hawthorne set outside America:

> No author, without a trial, can conceive of the difficulty of writing a romance about a country where there is no shadow, no antiquity, no mystery, no picturesque and gloomy wrong, nor anything but a commonplace prosperity, in broad and simple daylight, as is happily the case with my dear native land.[27]

The 'items' James provides are thus, in the first instance, designed to enumerate the resources unavailable to Hawthorne, what James, thinking of Hawthorne's *American Notebooks* (understood as 'a practical commentary upon this somewhat ominous text' and characterized by 'an extraordinary blankness' despite their author's 'large and healthy appetite for detail'), refers to as 'the lightness of the diet to which his observation was condemned'.[28] But James's quotation erases the awkwardness of Hawthorne's statement, leaving it as an apparently uncomplicated disposition of a 'broad and simple daylight' against the absence of 'shadow', 'antiquity', etc. His erasure is effected by deleting the sentences surrounding the quotation, sentences which set 'a sort of poetic or fairy precinct, where actualities would not be so terribly insisted upon as they are, and must needs be, in America' against the proposition that 'Romance and poetry, like ivy, lichens and wallflowers, need Ruin to make them grow.'[29]

Hawthorne's position in this Preface is by no means straightforward, and it is part of the function of James's erasure to render it more reductive than it is for the sake of his wider argument which will restore its complications in James's own terms. While he is not sure that Hawthorne 'had ever heard of Realism', he finds himself 'not fanciful' in suggesting that Hawthorne 'testifies to the sentiments of the society in which he flourished almost as pertinently (proportions observed) as Balzac and some of his descendents—MM. Flaubert and Zola—testify to the manners and morals of the French people'.[30] James's placing of Hawthorne in this company occurs within a page of a famous passage which suggests that his later catalogue of 'items' is precisely a catalogue of rhetorical resources (what Howells' review termed 'those novelistic "properties" '[31]) rather than cultural condemnation. The passage points the 'valuable moral' James derives from Hawthorne, a 'moral' which suggests the invidiousness of 'contrasting his proportions with those of a great civilisation':

> This moral is that the flower of art blooms only where the soil is deep, that it takes a great deal of history to produce a little literature, that it needs a complex social machinery to set a writer in motion.

This is of course only half of the 'moral' (the half which is so often attended to in isolation) and, too conveniently, it matches the later complaint about the absences in resource for the American writer. The gritty practicality of the second half drastically modifies any urge to make such a match:

> American civilisation has hitherto had other things to do than to produce flowers, and before giving birth to writers it has wisely occupied itself with providing something for them to write about.[32]

The sturdiness of James's recognition here, wonderfully undermining the metaphor of the first half of the passage, suggests how he is able to see Hawthorne, 'in spite of the absence of the realistic quality', as 'intensely and vividly local',[33] and, furthermore, appropriating such localism for his own purposes by reconstituting the conventions of realism.

James's appropriation of Hawthorne, particularly in his thoughts about *The House of the Seven Gables*, extends beyond a willingness to disorientate the comfort of conventional categories of writing and even beyond his insistence on possibilities for the reader's flexibility. The liberty proclaimed by Hawthorne's Preface in the 'moral' he offers for the story, and in the 'latitude' he wishes his form to maintain, enable James to describe Hawthorne as 'an American of Americans' which he defines by noting that, despite a sense of Hawthorne's conservatism, 'it is singular how often one encounters in his writings some expression of mistrust of old houses, old institutions, long lines of descent.'[34] Hawthorne's 'moral' ('the folly of tumbling down an avalanche of ill-gotten gold, or real estate, on the heads of an unfortunate posterity, thereby to maim and crush them' [35]) thus matches the 'latitude' he claims formally for himself and his reader. The debate about the ownership of property which constitutes the story itself elaborates this intersection of imaginative and material liberty. Brook Thomas has offered a good argument, premised on the American political system's founding on eighteenth-century models of impersonal authority freed from subjective interests and justified by invoking natural law, in which he claims:

> The status given a deed of property confirms the idea that an owner's authority to possess land is embodied in a text. A deed allows the person whose name is affixed to it to claim ownership of a piece of land. In a sense the document and the piece of property merge. The owner of the deed is the owner of the land. The owner's name coincides with the land. . . . But Hawthorne is acutely aware that sign and signifier do not coincide. Texts— including legal documents—have human authors and therefore derive their authority from human actions, not natural law. Furthermore, a document may as easily come from the irrational area of imagination as from the rational.

Thus, for Thomas, Hawthorne's story 'questions the impersonal, rational authority of a democracy's most sacred texts— its legal documents'.[36] Hawthorne's questioning of texts is, then, simultaneously a questioning of a material ideology, and it is within the intersection of the two that his concern with his own expression in the Preface needs to be read. It is also within this intersection that we need to read James's insertion by his study of the earlier author at the time of *Washington Square*'s alertness to the impositions of a bourgeois economy. Possession of property is the most material form of appropriation, of confining the freedom of others, particularly within a political system largely defined from the start by Lockean epistemology. The evanescence of portrayal, justified by Hawthorne and the object of both admiration and disquiet by James, itself has a function to resist the materiality that is the clearest product of such impersonal rationality. Impersonal rationality shares the guarantee of concealed authorship, fiction's sense of its own production; both are advertised as free from the excesses of the individual subjective imagination.

Hence both most appropriately rely upon the rhetoric of realism, the nomenclature not only of politics and law but also of science (the major sanction for realistic fiction's self-advertisement) which seeks its authority from the same rationality. While Judge Pyncheon is an appropriator of property, Dr. Sloper is an appropriator of linguistic capital.

3

James's interest in an author who concerned himself with, as it were, the hidden histories of the real through his restructuring of the relationship between imagination and felt experience, texts and con-texts, words and deeds, suggests that we need to think of the moment of *Washington Square* across the key issue which dominated both those periods of accelerated commercial expansion occasioning its action and its composition. This was the issue of money: specifically the debates about 'soft' and 'hard' money, paper and coin, which caused such intense public interest at the end of the Jacksonian era and during Reconstruction. By maintaining the tensile relationship between competing modes of style in *Hawthorne* and in *Washington Square*, the connections and disconnections between the rhetoric of imagination and that of realism, James is involved in an aesthetic arena that is especially appropriate to the field where debates about coined and paper money were conducted. Both raise the question of symbolism in general, the relation of words or signs to their objects, the immaterial to the material. James's displacements of style and the de-materialized centre of the novel's action mark a flexibility that is, in one sense, the more positive aspect of the instability in the hurly-burly of the commercial world whose main expression, money, is notoriously uncertain of its own status.

James's principal indictment of the bourgeois economy that figures the story's setting in the 1830s and 1840s and the period of its composition in the late 1870s is clearly in his characterization of Sloper, almost an archetype (if James thought in such terms) of the bourgeois temperament.[37] He offers Sloper as a man of science rather than as a man of business because the latter would be too reductive an invitation to enjoin 'fictional' and 'realist' comparisons. It would also elide the nexus of relationships that make possible the history of corporate market practice: relationships between abstract thought, numbers, science, technology and industry. Furthermore, the etymological relation between the 'species' and 'specimens' of scientific enquiry and the 'specie' of the money debates enables James obliquely to suggest the linguistic and ideological worlds in which he is willing to operate. Their shared Latin root means 'appearance', so that both belong to an epistemology which relies on the 'form', the 'look' of its objects at the risk of an unstable or distorting distance from the 'reality' of those objects. Paradoxically, in common usage both sets of terms acquire a strong empirical solidity, or specificity. The questions concerning representation raised by James's structuring of the Hawthorne/Balzac complex and by the money debates during the Jacksonian period and Reconstruction thus circumscribe an area in which our faith about the truth of our means of expression and exchange is to be tested through an interplay between the offices of aesthetics and those of money. Both, crucially, incorporate questions about freedom. Part of our cue may be taken from an argument by Marc Shell who is thinking about Poe's 'The Gold Bug', a story of the early 1840s:

> Credit or belief involves the very ground of aesthetic experience, and the same medium that seems to confer it in fiduciary money (bank-notes) and in scriptural money (created by the process of book-keeping) also seems to confer it in literature. That medium is writing. The apparently 'diabolical' 'interplay of money and mere writing to a point where the two be[come] confused' involves a general ideological development: the tendency of paper money to distort our 'natural' understanding of the relationship between symbols and things.[38]

The possibility of dis-credit, the gap between sign and substance, is thus a danger for both aesthetics and financial speculation. James is interested in that gap both as characteristic of the abstractions within the system of exchange and as a resource for writing which requires the real without the rhetoric of realism, which insists on imaginative free play. Again we recognize here, in the simultaneous positivity and negativity of the exercise, the risk James is taking.

As Shell acknowledges, 'America was the historical birth-place of widespread paper money in the Western World, and a debate about coined and paper money dominated American political discourse from 1825 to 1845.'[39] It was a debate which expressed itself most clearly in the political sphere through the argument about the banks and their appropriation of power. One of the best commentators on the issue, James Roger Sharp, has emphasized its politicization, claiming 'To Jackson and his hard-money followers, banks occupied privileged positions in society and exercised tremendous and virtually unchecked power', and that

> In an age dominated by an egalitarian spirit, the banks
> symbolized aristocratic privilege on the one hand, and the rapid
> and uncomfortable transition the country was undergoing from
> an agrarian to a commercial society on the other hand.[40]

Sharp also argues (and this is crucial for the historical positioning of *Washington Square*) that the bank debate reflected a wider argument about money which characterized the whole century,[41] so that by the time of the 'Gilded Age' itself, the money issue focused the political rhetoric of the Populists just as acutely as it had that of the Jacksonians.[42] The mania for land speculation during the 1830s was made possible to a great extent by the absence of a national paper currency; the circulating medium consisted of specie and the paper money issued by the hundreds of local banks. The Jacksonians, in attempting to control the inevitable instability which accompanied (and, indeed, in large part enabled) such speculation, viewed the banks as a threat to an advertisedly free and democratic society and maintained a faith in specie as 'a kind of perpetual and infallible balance wheel, regulating the workings of the banking system'. Specie, they felt, had 'an intrinsic and independent value of its own and could not depreciate as could paper money'.[43] Predictably then, the uncertain symbolism of paper money was countered by an argument for the seemingly more solid symbolism of gold and silver; we have the clear paradox of one form of abstraction competing with another on the contradictory grounds of its supposedly 'natural' materiality.

William Leggett, in a well-known essay on 'Equality' for the

New York *Evening Post* of 6 December 1834, categorically places the issue in terms of class struggle, the dominance which inhibits the freedom of others:

> The scrip nobility of this Republic have adopted towards the free people of this Republic the same language which the feudal barons and the despot who contested with them the power of oppressing the people used towards their serfs and villains, as they were opprobriously called.

Throughout, Leggett opposes what he variously terms 'would-be lordlings of the Paper Dynasty' and 'phantoms of the paper system' to the 'class which labours with its own hands'. Here is a clear application of the abstractions and distances based on a differentiation of intellectual and manual labour, a differentiation whose consequences become vividly apparent under the conditions of commodity production, of the shift from agrarian to industrial practice. The former group is constituted by those whose 'soul is wrapped up in a certificate of scrip or a bank note', and the only enemy facing the 'labouring classes' is the 'monopoly and a great paper system that grinds them to the dust'.[44] Jackson himself utilizes the same opposition in his Farewell Address of 1837: 'The agricultural, the mechanical, and the labouring classes have little or no share in the direction of the great moneyed corporations.'[45] Jackson's speeches in the 1830s exhibit succinctly the rhetoric of opposition to the questions of banks in general and paper money in particular, elaborating an immovable equation between banks, paper money and the abuse of democratic rights, along with manifest opportunity for fraud.[46] The instability of money characterizes the 1830s by means of its consequences: inflation and speculation. To control both, the administration issued the 'Specie Circular' in 1836 which provided that only gold and silver could be accepted by government agents in payment for public lands, the object of the most intense speculation by the middle of the decade. Against such appropriation of public property by means of uncertain currency, the Circular concludes:

> The principal objects of the President in adopting this measure being to repress alleged frauds, and to withhold any countenance or facilities in the power of the Government from the monopoly

of the public lands in the hands of speculators and capitalists, to the injury of the actual settlers in the new States, and of emigrants in search of new homes, as well as to discourage the ruinous extension of bank issues, and bank credits, by which those results are generally supposed to be promoted.[47]

Such was Jackson's distrust of the possibilities for making something out of nothing that he chose to devote virtually the whole of his Farewell Address in 1837 to the question of currency. Arguably it is the single most sustained attack on the 'evil' of paper money and the most rigorous justification of the 'constitutional currency' of gold and silver, of any public document. It begins by stressing the instability of contemporary conditions engendered by the untrustworthy symbolism of the paper medium:

> The paper system being founded on public confidence and having of itself no intrinsic value, it is liable to great and sudden fluctuations, thereby rendering property insecure and the wages of labor unsteady and uncertain. The corporations which create the paper money can not be relied upon to keep the circulating medium uniform in amount. In times of prosperity, when confidence is high, they are tempted by the prospect of gain or by the influence of those who hope to profit by it to extend their issues of paper beyond the bounds of discretion and the reasonable demands of business; and when these issues have been pushed on from day to day, until public confidence is at length shaken, then a reaction takes place, and they immediately withdraw the credits they have given, suddenly curtail their issues, and produce an unexpected and ruinous contraction of the circulating medium, which is felt by the whole community.[48]

The 'ebbs and flows' of the currency 'naturally' engender a 'wild spirit of speculation' which is morally harmful because it diverts attention from 'the sober pursuits of honest industry' and fosters an 'eager desire to amass wealth without labour'. The temptation to create something out of nothing 'inevitably' leads to an undermining of 'free institutions' and a corruption of authority by locating power in the hands of a privileged few. Jackson's sense of currency's impoverished symbolism, made particularly expressive in the obvious dangers of counterfeit notes, encourages him to articulate his argument in terms of

25

dominance and class,[49] and to see such counterfeits as encroaching upon human freedom by the 'natural associations' of the paper money system: 'monopoly and exclusive privileges'.[50]

The debates about money during the 1830s, the period in which Dr. Sloper architecturally appropriates a portion of New York land as an act of resistance against the city's commercial practices, thus marks the coalition of a series of social and aesthetic questions concerning the nature of symbolism, its material referents and its consequent rôle in redefined understandings about the nature of power and liberty. Political interest in the symbolism of money becomes revived during the years of Reconstruction and particularly during the 1870s, the decade which James ends by composing his study of *Hawthorne* and *Washington Square*.

The Coinage Act of February 1873 (nominated by latter-day Jacksonians as the 'crime of '73') put an end to the standard silver dollar. This demonetization of silver in effect redefined 'coin' as gold and added considerably to the size of taxes. The Specie Resumption Act of early 1875 deflated the currency until it was at a par with gold. These acts were seen by the populists as conferring a privileged monopoly on the banks 'which drew interest in gold on the government bonds the banks bought, and interest a second time on the notes the banks were then empowered to create and lend',[51] and the money question itself became paramount during the remainder of the decade which experienced one of the country's worst depressions.[52] A single statement in support of silver against gold by Democrat Richard Bland to Congress in August 1876 reveals the extent to which the Reconstruction debate on 'soft' versus 'hard' money continued the rhetoric of the 1830s. Bland was speaking on behalf of a bill to remonetize silver which he saw as 'a measure in the interest of the honest yeomanry of this country'. He saw the Public Credit Act of 1869 and the Coinage Act of 1873 which promised payment of government bonds in coin rather than the paper money with which they were originally purchased and then redefined 'coin' to be gold alone at the expense of silver, as being wholly in the interests of 'stock-jobbers and speculators'. To argue that the tax-payer must pay only in gold was 'robbery, nothing more, nothing less' since creditors would benefit enormously to the detriment of debtors.

> Because a measure is for once reported to this Congress that has within it a provision for the welfare of the people of the country against the corrupt legislation that has gone on here for the last sixteen years in the interest of the moneyed lords, it is here denounced as full of rascalities, and all this by the party that had perpetuated these injustices and brought corruption, fraud, infamy, and dishonour upon the country. . . . Mr. Speaker, the common people of the country cannot come to this Capitol. They are not here in your lobby. They are at home following the plow, cultivating the soil, or working in their workshops. It is the silvern and golden slippers of the money kings, the bankers and financiers, whose step is heard in these lobbies and who rule the finances of the country.[53]

Bland's statement relied for its effect on the full complex of ideas we associate with the Jacksonian position: the symbolism of money, the concentration of power and the consequent limiting of free voice and free action, and the division (admittedly nostalgic in expression) between intellectual labour (the paper world of the speculators) and manual labour (the concrete productivity of soil and workshop). The opposition of notes and specie during the earlier period has become recomposed into an opposition of silver and gold, but we should not assume that the apparent materiality of silver coin presents a more satisfactory symbolism than the more obviously immaterial bank note. Coinage also figures an abstract form of representation, as Sohn-Rethel has urged:

> A coin has stamped upon its body that it is to serve as a means of exchange and not as an object of use. . . . Its physical matter has visibly become a mere carrier of its social function. A coin, therefore, is a thing which conforms to the postulates of the exchange abstraction and is supposed, among other things, to consist of an immutable substance, a substance over which time has no power, and which stands in antithetic contrast to any matter found in nature.[54]

We might remind ourselves that Sohn-Rethel establishes a discernable historical connection between the evolution of coined money and abstractive thought in the establishment of a monetary economy in the early Greek states which created conditions for 'the capacity of conceptual reasoning in terms of abstract universals, a capacity which established full intellectual independence from manual labour'.[55] This connection exposes vividly the valorized oppositions on which capitalist economics and business practices rely and which in turn places the figuration of Sloper's bourgeois temperament most accurately: the abstract vocabulary of science, geometry, and cardinal numbers (in the form of monetized value) by which Catherine becomes available as a commodity.[56]

It is not so much the details of the debate about 'soft' and 'hard' money which concern us, but rather the fact that it has to do with modes of material expression, with questions interrogating the forms of solidity and meaning that may be attached to a crucial order of symbolism. And that symbolism may be seen to have a determinant place within the structures from which James wrote. The debate about money during the two periods in American history which witnessed such notable accelerations of industry and its allied commercial practices may be seen to share many of the features of an aesthetic concern to compose across James's readings of Hawthorne and Balzac, readings which probe the materiality of writing itself. The debate about money suggests, above all, the indeterminacy of currency's symbolism, of its rhetoric, and the inadequacy of an empiricist or mimetic base for evaluation and expression. These features become exacerbated by their visibility during a period of social instability, the realignment of class and interest groups, and economic depression immediately prior to the excesses of the Gilded Age. Treatises such as George M. Beard's *American Nervousness: Its Causes and Consequences* (New York, 1881) provided physiological evidence for the damaging impact of advanced industrial practices upon mind and body, offering, as it were, a material metaphor for those wider areas of instability which the present argument has attempted to locate.[57] And such work reminds us that the abstractions which so concern James in *Washington Square* are not to be confined to the further abstractive realm of ideas, but are material events which infect the very structures of feeling and behaviour.

## 4

It would be a mistake to view the instability of a world rapidly being revealed as a market-place for commodities solely in terms of the more apparent changes in the means of production. The development of the machines for industry should not be allowed to conceal the effects of concomitant changes in perceptions of money itself. Gerald T. Dunne has written well on this aspect of the transformations during the early nineteenth century of America's shift from an agrarian to an industrial economy:

> The rise of banking cut the fabric of tradition with an especial sharpness. Though the significance of the change was barely grasped and rarely articulated, the growing importance of banking amounted to a revolution in the traditional system of credit, which forced profound changes in outlook and values. Sharply challenged were the old agrarian views under which gold and silver, like fields and flocks, were the true essence of wealth. Rather, wealth was changing in form to the intangible—to paper bank notes, deposit entries on bank ledgers, shares in banks, in turnpikes, in canals, and in insurance companies. More important, perhaps, debt was no longer necessarily the badge of improvidence and misfortune. And from the creditor's point of view debt, in the form of bank notes or bank deposits became an instrument of power.[58]

Brook Thomas, in commenting on Dunne's description, has recognized the fuller abstraction and instability of what Dunne leaves as the 'intangible' form of wealth:

> In the new economy, the old theory that value was determined by the inherent properties of an object gave way to a subjective theory of value, in which the value of an object was determined by laws of supply and demand. In capital-poor but land-rich America, the land itself becomes just another commodity, fluctuating in value according to market conditions, the enterprise of developers, and the confidence games of speculators.[59]

Nowhere may the tissue of uncertainty be seen so clearly as within this paradox of a structure where economic power is measured by notes and documents, where the 'real' is constituted by the fabric of paper with all its inadequate and dangerous symbolism.[60] In the America of the 1840s, as Marc Shell tells us,

> comparisons were made between the way a mere shadow or piece of paper becomes credited as substantial money and the way that an artistic appearance is taken for the real thing by a willing suspension of disbelief.[61]

The paper that Dr. Sloper leaves behind as part of his 'explanation' to his patients is thus an 'inscrutable prescription' (p. 2), his only form of writing. We see here a clear contradiction of Sloper's office which mimes exactly the artistry of his science; it is a joke about the material appearance of writing that is to be taken seriously and literally. At both the fictional and material levels, 'inscrutable' writing requires further acts of re-composition to demystify its content, to make it publicly readable. The activity of forcing the signs of Sloper's writing to yield their substance, their meaning, is analogous both to the contemporary interrogation of the substance of money and its expression, and to the general habit of Sloper's profession, 'dividing people into classes, into types' (p. 101). Both these latter activities involve a willingness to believe in the accuracy of their modes of representation, and both specie and specimen rely on the 'look' of their expressions, sanctioned by a shared valorization of mathematics. In the case of money, particularly paper notes, we witness a dissociation of writing and its content which quite literally mimes the breach of intellectual and manual labour within the world conceived as an industrial market-place. The final conjunction which this equation enables is aesthetic; it is articulated in James's reading across of Hawthorne and Balzac at the time of *Washington Square*, as I have suggested, but it achieves its most famous expression in 1836, the year following the building of Sloper's house, in a statement from the chapter on 'Language' in Emerson's *Nature* (a text powerfully encoded by the transcendentalist response to America's first industrial revolution) where we find the question of literary and philosophical symbolism explicitly maintained through the figure of pecuniary fraud:

> A man's power to connect his thought with its proper symbol, and so to utter it, depends on the simplicity of his character,

that is, upon his love of truth and his desire to communicate it without loss. The corruption of man is followed by the corruption of language. When simplicity of character and the sovereignty of ideas is broken up by the prevalence of secondary desires, the desire of riches, of pleasure, of power, and of praise,—and duplicity and falsehood take place of simplicity and truth, the power over nature as an interpreter of the will is in a degree lost; new imagery ceases to be created, and old words are perverted to stand for things which are not; a paper currency is employed, when there is no bullion in the vaults. In due time the fraud is manifest, and words lose all power to stimulate the understanding or the affections.[62]

This statement occurs, of course, in that section of Emerson's essay which pervasively attempts to express the analogies of Swedenborgian 'Correspondence' in aesthetic terms: the ways in which the imagination frames and operates within the relationship between symbols and their referents. As a counter to the 'rotten diction' of a corrupted language, Emerson posits the urge to 'fasten words again to visible things' in order to create a 'picturesque language', a phrase where 'picturesque' is intended literally as a means to effect a 'commanding certificate' of truth. Hence he argues for the materiality of the images employed in true discourse, their 'emblematic' office within a system whereby 'the whole of nature is a metaphor of the human mind' exhibiting how the 'laws of moral nature answer to those of matter as face to face in a glass' or the 'axioms of physics translate the laws of ethics'.[63] Emerson's willingness to employ metaphors from science marks an arena shared by Sloper (and, indeed, by James himself in his disquisitions on the writing of fiction), but while Sloper's science characterizes an urge to privatization and dominance, that of Emerson functions as a metaphor to permit fluidity and interconnectedness. It is instructive that Emerson's essay on 'Swedenborg' in 1850 was capable of using technology (from, admittedly, the pre-industrial era) to maintain the sturdiness of Swedenborg's metaphysics. James felt incapable of Emerson's confidence in an 'exact relation' of symbol to its substance, but he well remembered with affection, in his essay of 1887, Emerson's reading of the 'Boston Hymn' which clearly suggested the exploitative economic base of the concern with symbols in *Nature*. The occasion was the meeting in the Boston Music Hall in 1863 to celebrate Lincoln's signing of the proclamation which freed the Southern slaves. James recalls the 'immense effect' with which Emerson's 'beautiful voice' pronounced the lines:

> Pay ransom to the owner
> And fill the bag to the brim.
> Who is the owner? The slave is owner,
> And ever was. Pay *him*![64]

Whereas what Emerson elsewhere termed 'nature's geometry' figures a decided consolation for the transcendentalist temperament, James's more acute geometry points crisis and instability on behalf of the allied areas of science, commerce, aesthetics, and human relationships. It is in this sense that the silence which so awkwardly expresses the commodification of Catherine has its double function to register a resistance to the commercial world and to betoken the paralysis of genuine intercourse. It is also in this sense that we are invited to read a curious figure on behalf of James's own activity of composition.

The figure occurs at the beginning of Chapter Ten when Townsend, reluctantly, visits Catherine at home following his unspoken argument with her father. He is received on Catherine's own choice of ground, a 'New York drawing-room' which is given a temporal description as 'furnished in the fashion of fifty years ago'. In other words, its furnishing belongs to a pre-industrial era, but by this stage in the novel we have lost our sense of the insistent specificity of time which marks its opening; such temporal detail is non-existent in the main action of the story which underlines its occurrence here as indicative of the nostalgia that Catherine never utters. We are then presented with a more definite description (the only one of its kind in the whole novel) of a particular item: as Townsend begins his assertions, he glances at

> the long, narrow mirror which adorned the space between the two windows, and which had at its base a little gilded bracket covered by a thin slab of white marble, supporting in its turn a backgammon board folded together in the shape of two

volumes, two shining folios inscribed in letters of greenish gilt, *History of England.* (p. 70)

Opened up here is a play between the loosely novelistic gesture of 'fifty years ago' (matching that of the story's own opening sentence, 'During a portion of the first half of the present century, and more particularly during the latter part of it . . .' which in itself signals a cavalier free-play with the specificity of time), denoting, presumably, an American past, and the embellished masquerade of a different past, that of England which, within a more domestic history, provided the 'germ' of the story.[65] It is a play which receives attention in the correspondence with Howells about the 'items of high civilisation' in *Hawthorne* from which James proposes *Washington Square* as a determinedly 'truly American' tale.

The mirror would inevitably reflect not only Townsend's self-conscious 'glance' (the 'gilt' in its turn rather crudely punning the guilt of his occasion), but also the surface of the *History* itself, a precious object whose only reality, concealed by its surface, is a game whose chance and hazard are further concealed by the geometry of its rules. The description distances itself from the rhetoric of novelistic expression (measured in part, for example, by James's description of Mrs. Montgomery's house at the beginning of Chapter Fourteen) and has no local function to expand our sense of character or place. It merely lies there in the text as an abstracted item which contributes nothing to the narrative; it is sheer decoration. Neither is it an item of more fanciful or mysterious allegory such as we might find in Hawthorne. The mirror's surface (one of the most important of Jamesian value-terms) is literally mimetic, positioned so that it reflects not the vista of the outside world beyond the two windows which frame it (a framing of an internal view by the possibilities for an external view which thereby cancel a traditional figure for mimesis), but only an imitation text. James's self-regarding irony here suggests the catalogue of propositions about writing through which *Washington Square* negotiates its exploratory course. It permits only one form of material solidity, the 'gilt' letters inscribing the *History* (sustained, in both senses, by the slab of marble on its 'gilded' bracket) that provide a reminder of the economic conditions enabling the building of houses in Washington Square and the writing of novels about them.

## 5

By way of conclusion, I want, briefly, to consider the situation of Morris Townsend, partly because he has received such a uniformly bad press of the kind which elides his significance in the novel,[66] and partly to realign that unsympathetic treatment in order to locate him more concretely within the social historicism of *Washington Square*. Townsend needs, quite simply, to be understood as having a definite rôle to play in James's explicit critique of New York's bourgeois economy, regarding its nascence in the accelerated commercial practices of the 1830s and 1840s from the point of view of its more expressive characteristics in the late 1870s. To this end, it is a mistake merely to dismiss Townsend through the stereotypes of a heartless lover or an interloper, since such categorization inevitably seals him off from the material history that is probed by the novel's general project. It is to the presentation of a material history that the following remarks propose to return Townsend: to the social and economic forces through which the novel realizes itself.

We may begin by noting the proximity of Townsend's features to those of Dr. Sloper who is himself offered as almost an archetype (not that James would deploy the word) of the bourgeois temperament which sustains a view of the world as a market-place for commodities by a balanced, rational discourse authorized by the types of science and the precepts of mathematics. Like Sloper, Townsend, when under the pressure of choosing his appropriate strategy, is capable of viewing Catherine, and indeed himself, as economic quantities,[67] and of figuring their situation in mathematical terms.[68] Sloper's tone is particularly apparent in the patronizing irony of Townsend's voice during his second secret meeting with Mrs. Penniman (pp. 154–57), and she is later, predictably, to acclaim the 'charm' of what she recognizes as his 'formula' for giving up Catherine (p. 205). Townsend's final letter to Catherine, explaining this decision, invokes a view of themselves thoroughly within a notion of scientific computation as 'innocent but philosophic victims of a great social law' (p. 232). Earlier, having wished that Catherine would 'hold fast' to her relationship with himself (p. 116), he rapidly appropriates Sloper's own determinant hope that she will 'stick' (pp. 150, 155), a term which, foremost in Sloper's lexicon of his daughter, points exactly the paralysed world maintained by both science and business practice.[69]

Townsend's approximation to the abstractive sensibility of Sloper structures, however, only part of his force in the novel. He is given the first item of direct speech as the action of the narrative begins in Chapter Four: 'What a delightful party! What a charming house! What an interesting family! What a pretty girl your cousin is!' (p. 22). Here, rushed together, are the discrete units for the more expanded discourse of polite conversation. The speech approximates the non-dialogical tenor of Sloper's linguistic manner but is clearly less dominating; the difference is that Townsend's condensed utterance (with its implicit reluctance for discursive lee-way) marks his distance from, and perhaps his awkwardness within, the social occasion. The observations he makes are, we are told, 'of no great profundity', but from Catherine's stance he goes on 'to say many other things in the same comfortable and natural manner' (p. 22). Her own social awkwardness leads her to see his locquaciousness as oddly paradoxical:

> Catherine had never heard anyone—especially any young man—talk just like that. It was the way a young man might talk in a novel; or, better still, in a play, on a stage, close before the footlights, looking at the audience, and with everyone looking at him. . . . And yet Mr. Townsend was not like an actor; he seemed so sincere, so natural. (pp. 24–5)

This paradoxical mixture of the theatrical and the natural is picked up by Townsend himself a little later during the first conversation he has alone with Catherine in Washington Square. Revealingly, it is offered in the context of one of the most important Jamesian tenets—the liberty of individual perception:

> He had been to places that people had written books about, and they were not a bit like the descriptions. To see for yourself— that was the great thing; he always tried to see for himself. He

35

had seen all the principal actors—he had been to all the best
theatres in London and Paris. But the actors were always like
the authors—they always exaggerated. He liked everything to
be natural. (p. 41)

Nevertheless, we know his naturalness to be the main
feature of his social artifice. Sloper himself is shortly to make a
joke about the same topic; when Mrs. Almond argues that 'the
thing is for Catherine to see it', he replies: 'I will present her
with a pair of spectacles!' (p. 53). The abstractions of the novel
are such that naturalness itself becomes enlisted on behalf of a
determinant artifice; John Lucas, in disagreeing with Richard
Poirier's reading of *Washington Square* as a play with 'a melodramatic fairy-tale', points us in the right direction when he
notes:

> if the characters *do* become like stock types in stage melodrama
> and fairy tale . . . it is because they see themselves called on to
> play parts created by their self-conscious awareness of what
> their society requires of them.[70]

Lucas's argument suggests the linguistic disablement of social
conditions, the conditions of accelerated industrial and commercial enterprise which impose the abstract structure of
commodity exchange, breached from use, upon human relationships. Catherine is unable to figure Townsend's conversation in any but theatrical terms because it is so unfamiliar to
her and she has no other available resource; she acknowledges
an artifice so unreal by comparison, let us say, with that of
Mrs. Penniman,[71] that it seems a form of the natural. Sloper
displays his control of the idea when he informs Townsend
that 'I am not a father in an old-fashioned novel' (p. 90).

If any single word dominates *Washington Square*, it is 'natural'
or its variants. And, substantially, by far the largest number of
its occasions refers to Townsend. It provides the theme of his
first open tribute to Catherine: ' "That's what I like you for;
you are so natural. Excuse me," he added; "you see I am
natural myself" ' (p. 41). His sense of his 'fine natural parts'
(p. 159) combined with a confidence of manner form the basis
of his physical attractiveness to which not only Catherine but
even Sloper respond. Despite the fact that such naturalness
constitutes a large part of his social artifice, there is a curious

way in which it may be read in its own terms. To dismiss Townsend as a social climber or a fortune-hunter serves only to fix him too unproblematically. What is insisted upon is his sense of being out of place; he feels 'a great stranger in New York. It was his native place; but he had not been there for many years' (p. 24), and Catherine's early impression, coupled with her theatrical metaphors, is that 'He's more like a foreigner' (p. 33). His main feature is mobility, having travelled extensively abroad prior to the commencement of the story; travels to which he returns after his failure with Catherine. We know little of his family history, save that he has a sister in reduced circumstances, that he has been 'wild' in his youth (a notoriously indeterminate term), and that his branch of the Townsends is not 'of the reigning line' (p. 44). The interstitial social area in which James locates Townsend is, of course, characteristic of a period of intense development and change whereby existing class-lines become blurred and the great effort is to move beyond them, to articulate some proper social shape. The problem for the artist, as Forster is to encounter with Leonard Bast, Lawrence with Paul Morel, and, to a lesser extent, Dreiser with Clyde Griffiths during a later period of accelerated transformations, is to render this mobility of social place; how is such newness to be described in the world, this new style which is invariably at odds with existing social styles?

When she is told that Townsend has no 'business', Catherine expresses the surprise of one who had never heard of a young man 'in this situation' (p. 34). At the top of Sloper's list of inquiries about Townsend is the question 'What is his profession?' (p. 45). In the work of a writer where we rarely find anyone having to suffer the iniquities of a 'profession' in its full material sense, we are especially alert to this insistence in *Washington Square*. It is, after all, a novel which begins with an extraordinarily complex diagnosis of 'profession', that of Sloper which provides the entire social and economic base on which its history rests. James's monograph on Hawthorne, composed immediately prior to the novel, makes a famous statement on the subject:

> It is not too much to say that even to the present day it is a considerable discomfort in the United States not to be 'in

37

business'. The young man who attempts to launch himself in a career that does not belong to the so-called practical order; the young man who has not, in a word, an office in the business-quarter of the town, with his name painted on the door, has but a limited place in the social system, finds no particular bough to perch on.[72]

The 'profession' that concerns James principally here is, of course, that of author and its social reception, but his stress on the necessity of being 'in business' remains valuable on its own; it is the distinguishing feature of Townsend's condition that, in the social and commercial world of lower Manhattan, he 'finds no particular bough to perch on'. The absence of a 'profession' is, then, a prime cipher of the mobility and indeterminacy which circumscribes Townsend's 'naturalness' as a tactic against the styles of Washington Square. His position is 'natural' in the sense that there exists no available societal vocabulary whereby it may be given expression; it has no name.

The kind of job that we are told Townsend eventually acquires is particularly germane to the period in which the novel is set.[73] He gains a partnership with a 'commission merchant' (p. 183). His function thereby is to mediate between manufacturers and the selling of their products in foreign markets, and, as such, the commission merchant is probably 'the most important figure in the foreign trade organisation of both the United States and Great Britain'. This is particularly true of the state of New York for which the Census of 1840 lists 1,044 commission houses as contrasted with 469 commercial houses.[74] What is illuminating about this choice of profession for Townsend goes beyond its specific historical typicality; it incorporates that form of agency which is disengaged simultaneously from the systems of production and the immediate systems of selling. In other words, it exposes a most apposite figure for the forms of disengagement and abstraction which characterize a period of rapid industrial development, those very forms which in turn provide the focus for James's critique of bourgeois economy, his sense of how they infect the structures of feeling constituting the liberty of human relationships. The world of Townsend's eventual 'profession' (like that of his cousin, the 'stout young stockbroker' who is the brief spokesman for the city's transformations (pp. 31–2) as the novel's only other businessman) is a paper world, wholly devoid of material process or any real contact with productivity, and, as paper, is reminiscent of the alarming instability of that final abstraction, money itself, an issue which dominated American political thought during both the period of the novel's action and the period of its composition. The location of Townsend's supposed office in 'a place peculiarly and unnaturally difficult to find' (p. 201) mimes exactly the shadowy nature of the job itself and, more generally, his membership of a new, emerging, changing class.[75]

To read Townsend as a social climber is to do no more than incorporate the partiality of Sloper's own typology; he presents a threat, but its real danger is that it cannot be fully formulated, not only because of his uncertain social positioning but because of a specific feature of Sloper's bourgeois temperament. As Roland Barthes notes, it is a feature of the bourgeois mind (and, we may add, of the exchange relation which characterizes the dispersal of commodities, the defining objects of the bourgeois universe) that it obscures 'the ceaseless making of the world'.[76] What Townsend's mobility and his interstitial placing threaten above all is exactly an exposure of the 'making' of the world via his putative progress through it. To resist (to paralyse) Townsend is, in effect, to erase the 'making' of Sloper's own location because the bourgeois idea of itself is, in Barthes's definition, of 'the social class which does not want to be named'.[77] The potential interruption of Townsend marks precisely the path Sloper himself has followed. Townsend thus most profoundly threatens nothing so crude as Sloper's own position, or even the financial spoilation of his daughter, but the revelation of change, of alterability, of moving beyond the confines of his classification. His fluidity, his 'naturalness', proposes to dissolve the geometry by which Sloper and the Square are maintained paradoxically against the 'mighty uproar' of 'trade' and the 'base uses of commerce' (pp. 16–17), those disturbances which themselves seek sanction from the abstractions of science and mathematics. Sloper's treatment of Townsend is a paradigm of the conservative resistance to the new, of the bourgeois disguising (or deliberate blinding) of itself. We may see, then, that Townsend becomes the novel's less obvious victim and, more clearly, the victim of the period's transformations as he struggles within its simultaneous promise of economic amelioration and its damnation of those whom its accelerations leave behind.

## NOTES

I am grateful to my colleagues Martin Crawford and Robert Garson, and to Nicola Bradbury of the University of Reading, for their advice during the composition of this essay.

1. I. F. A. Bell, ' "This Exchange of Epigrams": Commodity and Style in *Washington Square*', *Journal of American Studies* (forthcoming).
2. Henry James, *Washington Square* (Macmillan and Co., London, 1881), p. 17. All subsequent references will be included parenthetically in the body of the text. In the short story, 'An International Episode', published shortly before *Washington Square* (in the *Cornhill Magazine*, December, 1878–January, 1879), James presents a clear picture of the pressures within New York's commercial world.
3. Mrs. Penniman's travesties of what is usually a prime value in James, the imaginative faculty, suggest accurately her social place. Mary Doyle Springer notes: 'Aunt Penniman exists to reveal by her acts the real heart of darkness: that in such a milieu women ("the imperfect sex") not only cooperate passively with what the eithics of a paternalistic society makes necessary, but also cooperate actively in exploiting each other because that is what the whole social system gives them to do, and gives them little else to do if they are unmarried' (*A Rhetoric of Literary Character: Some Women of Henry James* (Chicago, 1978), p. 81).
4. Millicent Bell, 'Style as Subject: *Washington Square*', *Sewanee Review*, LXXXIII.1 (Winter 1975), 23.
5. Millicent Bell suggests: 'If *Washington Square* derives from *Eugénie Grandet* it may also be said to come out of "Rappacini's Daughter"' (loc. cit., p. 24). We might note, on behalf of James's choice of profession for Sloper, that Hawthorne's fictions are well staffed by scientific figures who are not only felt to be cruel with respect to human affections but arrogant in their distortions of nature: to Rappaccini we may add Aylmer, Ethan Brand, Dr. Heidegger and Roger Chillingworth.
   For bibliographical information on the relationship between *Washington Square* and Hawthorne's works, see Thaddeo K. Babiiha, *The James-Hawthorne Relation* (Boston, 1980), pp. 264–66.
6. See I. F. A. Bell, loc. cit.
7. Such an urge is tested, for example, when Sloper interrogates first Catherine and then Townsend on the timing of their first meeting. They

are both inexplicably evasive (*Washington Square*, ed. cit., pp. 78 and 84), and the novelistic reader is impelled to question their lie over so trivial and unthreatening a detail.

This issue has recently been investigated, albeit rather one-sidedly, by William W. Stowe, *Balzac, James and the Realistic Novel* (Princeton, 1983).

8. Alfred Sohn-Rethel, *Intellectual and Manual Labour: A Critique of Epistemology* (1970), trans. Martin Sohn-Rethel (London, 1978), pp. 56 and 49.

9. See J. L. Winter, 'The Chronology of James's *Washington Square*', *Notes and Queries*, N.S. XXVIII.5 (October 1981), 426–28.

10. James's worries about novelistic conventions are summarized early in his writing life when he concludes his anonymous review of *Middlemarch* with a well-known question: 'It sets a limit, we think, to the development of the old-fashioned English novel. Its diffuseness, on which we have touched, makes it too copious a dose of pure fiction. If we write novels so, how shall we write History?' (The review was first published in the *Galaxy* (March 1873); my quotation is taken from the reprint in *Nineteenth-Century Fiction*, VIII.3 (December 1953), 170.) Towards the end of that life, such worries are to an extent allayed by a faith in the dramatic 'objectivity' he defines in his Preface to *The Awkward Age*: 'The divine distinction of the act of a play—and a greater than any other it easily succeeds in arriving at—was, I reasoned, in its special, its guarded objectivity. This objectivity, in turn, when achieving its ideal, came from the imposed absence of that "going behind," to compass explanations and amplifications, to drag out odds and ends from the "mere" storyteller's great property-shop of aids to illusion. . . .' (*The Art of the Novel*, ed. R. P. Blackmur (1934; New York, 1962), pp. 110–11).

11. The tensions constituting this complex are, indeed, apparent in Hawthorne's own investigations into the notions of power and authority concomitant upon his craft, particularly in the tales and in the Prefaces. Recently, Brook Thomas has provided an acute analysis of Hawthorne's deployment of the Romance form in '*The House of the Seven Gables*: Reading the Romance of America', *P.M.L.A.*, XCVII.2 (March 1982), 195–211.

12. Leo Bersani, 'The Jamesian Lie', *Partisan Review*, XXXVI.1 (Winter 1969), 54.

13. Ibid., 57–8. More recently, Bersani has extended his account of James's efforts to deconstruct the novelistic pretensions of fiction to suggest their political effect: 'Because of James's remarkable indifference to that diversification of behaviour by which other novelists seek to convince us that their characters have more than verbal authority, his novels demystify literature's claim to be a reflector of nonliterary life and they diagram the specific mechanisms of power when its exercise is limited to verbal exchanges.' These literary diagrams, by virtue of their very removal from novelistic furniture, thus have 'the exemplary value of demonstrating that transactions of power always involve communications,

and that these communications frequently take the form of equivocal donations of knowledge.' And here lies the core of James's political function: 'literature, exactly because it is power enacted uniquely as a form of organized knowledge, can serve the politically useful rôle of dramatizing the nothingness of all epistemological fictions' ('The Subject of Power', *Diacritics* (Fall 1977), 10–12). I am not absolutely clear what Bersani intends by 'nothingness' here but, as applied to James, it would make sense to read it as an implication of James's stress on imaginative variousness: an effect of interruption whereby the world is revealed as constructed, and, beyond the field of its historical production, no one fiction has any more privileged access to a transcendental authenticity than any other—no more than a purely private guarantee of the 'real'.

14. See Brook Thomas, loc. cit.
15. Tzvetan Todorov, *The Poetics of Prose* (1971), trans. Richard Howard (Oxford, 1977), p. 150. Todorov's account of what he terms 'the quest for an absolute and absent cause' (p. 145) in Jamesian narrative (an account which is little recognized by the commentators) is extremely perceptive about this important topic, but ultimately relies on a primacy of the 'unreal' (or psychic reality) over the 'real' which marks a distortive and potentially reductive reading of the complex which the present essay attempts to maintain as a more tensile construct.
16. My quotations are taken from *The Centenary Edition of the Works of Nathaniel Hawthorne*, ed. William Charvat, Roy Harvey Pearce, Claude M. Simpson (Columbus, Ohio, 1965), pp. 1–3.
17. The reverse is true of James, but the effect is the same, as Taylor Stoehr notes: 'The notebooks in which James stored his materials are filled with plots and the making of plots—relationships, encounters, sketches of action. There is little interest in facts or truths observed from life, and the stories he hears at dinner-parties are chiefly regarded as "germs" for his imagination to work with, the less of the actuality known the better' ('Words and Deeds in *The Princess Casamassima*', *E.L.H.*, XXXVII.1 (March 1970), 132). By the time of the New York Edition, James was capable of being coy about even his 'germs' (of which he makes great play at the beginning of his Preface to *The Awkward Age*), but, nevertheless, the notebooks, more so than his published essays, provide good evidence of James's interest in the *pattern* of things prior to the more familiar statements in the Prefaces.
18. Henry James, *Hawthorne* (1879), ed. Tony Tanner (London, 1967), p. 119.
19. Ibid., p. 127.
20. Ibid., p. 126.
21. Ibid., p. 129.
22. Ibid., p. 88.
23. Leon Edel, *The Life of Henry James*, 2 vols. (Harmondsworth, 1977), Vol. I, p. 595.
24. *Henry James Letters*, ed. Leon Edel (Cambridge, Mass., 1975), Vol. II, p. 268.
25. *Hawthorne*, ed. cit., p. 55.

26. *Letters*, ed. cit., Vol. II, p. 268.
27. *Hawthorne*, ed. cit., p. 54.
28. Idem.
29. My quotations are taken from the *Centenary Edition* (see note 18) of *The Marble Faun*, 1968, p. 3.
30. *Hawthorne*, ed. cit., p. 24.
31. W. D. Howells, 'James's *Hawthorne*', *Atlantic Monthly* (February 1880); reprinted in *W. D. Howells as Critic*, ed. Edwin H. Cady (1973), p. 54.
32. *Hawthorne*, ed cit., p. 23.
33. Idem.
34. Ibid., pp. 123–24.
35. Nathaniel Hawthorne, *The House of the Seven Gables*, ed. cit., p. 2.
36. Brook Thomas, '*The House of the Seven Gables*: Reading the Romance of America', *P.M.L.A.*, XCVII.2 (March 1982), 199.
37. See I. F. A. Bell, loc. cit. I have principally in mind here the models for balance within bourgeois behaviour offered by Roland Barthes, 'Myth Today', *Mythologies* (1957), trans. Annette Lavers (St. Albans, 1973), and Theodor Adorno and Max Horkheimer, *Dialectic of Enlightenment* (1947), trans. John Cumming (London, 1979). Barthes writes of an 'intellectual equilibrium based on recognised places' whereby 'reality is first reduced to analogues; then it is weighed; finally, equality having been ascertained, it is got rid of.' It is here that 'one flees from an intolerable reality, reducing it to two opposites which balance each other only inasmuch as they are purely formal, relieved of all their specific weight.' Material process is erased in favour of a 'final equilibrium' which 'immobilizes values, life, destiny, etc.' so that 'one no longer needs to choose, but only to endorse' (pp. 152–53). For Adorno and Horkheimer, 'Bourgeois society is ruled by equivalence. It makes the dissimilar comparable by reducing it to abstract quantities.' Such 'equivalence' is seen to 'dominate bourgeois justice and commodity exchange' (p. 7) as a form of abstraction which characterizes not only the exchange relation of commodities, the determining objects of the bourgeois world, but also the distortive function of the main feature whereby the bourgeois advertises itself, so that 'the bourgeois ideal of naturalness intends not amorphous nature, but the virtuous mean' (p. 31). It is not accidental that one of the more problematical of the novel's terms is 'natural' itself as applied, predominantly, to Morris Townsend.
38. Marc Shell, 'The Gold Bug', *Genre*, XIII.1 (Spring 1980), 18.
39. Ibid., 15.
40. James Roger Sharp, *The Jacksonians versus the Banks* (New York, 1970), pp. 5 and 6. For further discussions of the Jacksonian bank debate, see Bray Hammond, *Banks and Politics in America: From the Revolution to the Civil War* (Princeton, 1957); Marvin Meyers, *The Jacksonian Persuasion* (Stanford, 1957); Robert V. Remini, *Andrew Jackson and the Bank War* (New York, 1967); Peter Temin, *The Jacksonian Economy* (New York, 1969).
41. 'The Jacksonian attack on the banks was but a single episode in an

43

extended debate over banking, credit, and currency that lasted throughout the nineteenth century. The rhetoric of the Jacksonians and their
fears were similar in tone and content to those expressed earlier by John
Taylor of Caroline [the clearest and most persuasive exponent of
Jeffersonian principles, always the ground for the century's agrarian
argument] in the early nineteenth century and nearly a century later by
Populist leaders. All were representatives of an agrarian society who felt
that their moral values were being eroded away by the commercialization
of society and the quickening tempo of industry' (Sharp, op. cit., p. 6).

42. 'Throughout the century there was a fervently held belief that privately
issued paper money was an exploitative device by which capitalists and
bankers could control prices and the money supply. This, in turn, it was
argued, gave these special citizens enormous political and economic
power and made a mockery of a society that emphasized equal rights for
all and special privileges for none' (Sharp, op. cit., p. 8).

43. Sharp, op. cit., pp. 9–18.

44. William Leggett, 'Equality', *Evening Post*, 6 December 1834; reprinted in
*Builders of American Institutions. Readings in United States History*, ed. Frank
Freidel and Norman Pollack (Chicago, 1966), pp. 157–58.

45. Andrew Jackson, 'Farewell Address', 1837; reprinted in *Builders of
American Institutions*, ed. cit., p. 156.

46. At the very beginning of his Bank Veto in 1832, Jackson expresses 'the
belief that some of the powers and privileges possessed by the existing
bank are unauthorised by the constitution, subversive of the rights of the
States, and dangerous to the liberties of the people' (reprinted in *Select
Documents Illustrative of the History of the United States 1776–1861*, ed.
William Macdonald (New York and London, 1898), p. 262). His Fifth
Annual Message of 1833 reiterates the warning of constitutional infringement by offering what he terms 'unquestionable proof' that the Bank of
the United States had been converted into a 'permanent electioneering
machine' as a justification for his removal of the Bank's deposits: 'In this
point of the case, the question is distinctly presented, whether the people
of the United States are to govern through representatives chosen by
their unbiased suffrages, or whether the money and power of a great
corporation are to be secretly exerted to influence their judgement, and
control their decisions' (reprinted in *Select Documents* . . ., ed. cit., pp. 301–
2). The point is repeated in his Sixth Annual Message of 1834 where,
condemning the Bank as 'the scourge of the people', Jackson urges that
'measures be taken to separate the Government entirely from an institution so mischievious to the public prosperity, and so regardless of the
Constitution and laws' (reprinted in *Select Documents* . . ., ed. cit., p. 320).

47. 'Specie Circular', 1836; Reprinted in *Select Documents* . . ., ed. cit.,
pp. 328–29.

48. Jackson, 'Farewell Address', loc. cit., pp. 154–55.

49. 'Some of the evils which arise from this system of paper press with
peculiar hardship upon the class of society least able to bear it. A portion
of this currency frequently becomes depreciated or worthless, and all of
it is easily counterfeited in such a manner as to require peculiar skill and

much experience to distinguish the counterfeit from the genuine note. These frauds are most generally perpetrated in the smaller notes, which are used in the daily transactions of ordinary business, and the losses occasioned by them are commonly thrown upon the laboring classes of society, whose situation and pursuits put it out of their power to guard themselves from these impositions, and whose daily wages are necessary for their subsistence' (ibid., p. 155).

50. Ibid., p. 157.

51. Walter T. K. Nugent, *The Money Question During Reconstruction* (New York, 1967), pp. 16–17.

52. Nugent notes: 'No one realized in 1865, but money was destined to become the chief perennial issue in national politics for over thirty years. . . . Its peculiar dimensions were established in almost all important ways during the Reconstruction years, from 1867 to 1879' (op. cit., pp. 21–2). Richard Hofstadter similarly claims: 'a whole generation of Americans were embroiled from the 1870s to the 1890s in the argument over silver. To the combatants of that era, silver and gold were not merely precious metals but precious symbols, the very substance of creeds and faiths which continued long afterward to have meaning for men living on the echoes of nineteenth-century orthodoxies' ('Free Silver and the Mind of "Coin" Harvey', reprinted in Hofstadter's *The Paranoid Style in American Politics* (1964; New York, 1967), pp. 238–39). Hofstadter's essay deals mainly with the 'Free Silver' campaigns of the 1890s, but offers a brief and readable account of monetary events during the 1870s (pp. 250–57). Irwin Unger, in one of the best discussions of the subject, has argued: 'In the decade and a half following Appomattux, national finance absorbed more of the country's intellectual and political energy than any other public question except Reconstruction' (*The Greenback Era: A Social and Political History of American Finance 1865–1879* (1964; Princeton, 1967), p. 3). Unger may be paired with Robert P. Sharkey (*Money, Class, and Party: An Economic Study of Civil War and Reconstruction* (1959; Baltimore, 1967) as providing the most detailed and reliable guide to the history of money during the period. Both also offer excellent bibliographies of the massive literature concerned with the subject.

53. Quoted in Nugent, op. cit., pp. 96–7. In addition to Bland's catalogue of dominating moneyed interests, we might note the expansion of the corporate device during Reconstruction. Jan W. Dietrichson has claimed: 'In use before the Civil War mainly as a means to accumulate capital for turnpikes, railroads, and banks, the corporation rapidly became the dominant force of business organization in the post-war years, making easier the raising of large amounts of capital. It gave continuity of control, easy expansion of capital, concentration of administrative authority, diffusion of responsibility, and the privileges and immunities of a "person" in law and in interstate activities' (*The Image of Money in the American Novel of the Gilded Age* (New York, 1969), p. 11). Such abstractive 'diffusion of responsibility' and 'immunities' would have been anathema to James who always hated institutional or organized intrusions

into private liberties. It is instructive that the only other novels he wrote which explicitly advertise a social history, *The Bostonians* (usefully, from the point of view of *Washington Square*, set in the 1870s) and *The Princess Casamassima*, are both concerned with the impositions by organizations (of feminists and of anarchists respectively) upon personal freedom. His concern extends to language; Taylor Stoehr, on behalf of *The Princess Casamassima*, paraphrases an argument from *The Theories of Anarchy and Law* by James's friend, Henry B. Brewster: 'Man must learn to enjoy this freedom from settled formulations. He must accept the responsibility for creating reality through speech, and must refrain from the fetishism of names that embalms life with words' ('Words and Deeds in *The Princess Casamassima*', *E.L.H.*, XXXVII.1 (March 1970), 130). Diagrammatically here we have the debate of Hawthorne versus Balzac, albeit in somewhat reductive form since the issue was never so clearly presentable to James. In a paradoxical way, we might want to consider Verena Tarant's 'natural' and 'spontaneous' oratory in *The Bostonians* as belonging to the same field of inquiry as Catherine Sloper's silence, since Verena's voice, too, is made subject to the pressures of abstract organization; her voice is offered as a form of pure utterance whose contents are rendered vacuous by the rhetoric of Olive Chancellor's privileged ideals. Catherine's silence and Verena's utterance are equally emptied of material process and paralysed by domestic versions of institutions.

54. Sohn-Rethel, op. cit., p. 59.
55. Ibid., p. 60.
56. See I. F. A. Bell, loc. cit. B. J. Williams has offered a good argument for seeing Sloper as a 'hard' money figure (associated with the solidity of the earlier Republican values evinced by Jefferson and Adams who recognized the 'cheat' of any discrepancy between a bank bill and the quantity of gold and silver which sanctioned it) and Townsend as belonging to the world of 'soft' money, the paper world of extended credit: see '*Washington Square*: Fiction as History', unpubl. B.A. Dissertation, University of Keele, 1983.
57. Irwin Unger, on a more technical model, has seen this instability in terms of specific confusions, claiming an absence of consensus for the very definition itself of money: 'Some writers held that only gold and silver coin, bank notes, and government paper that performed exchanges and passed from hand to hand functioned as money; others said bank credits and deposits also qualified. They disagreed, too, over the significance of the interest bearing debt, much of which circulated as money between interest paying periods. From the point of view of a modern economist the whole financial discussion has an air of unreality' (*The Greenback Era: A Social and Political History of American Finance 1865–1879* (1964; Princeton, 1968), p. 36).
58. Gerald T. Dunne, *Justice Story and the Rise of the Supreme Court* (New York, 1970), pp. 142–43.
59. Brook Thomas, '*The House of the Seven Gables*: Hawthorne's Legal Story'. I am grateful to Professor Thomas for permission to quote from the typescript of his as yet unpublished essay.

60. Marc Shell has noted how 'paper counted for nothing as a commodity and was thus "insensible" in the economic system of exchange' (loc. cit., p. 15). This suggests the inadequacy of its symbolism, and we may add that its danger, beyond local effects such as counterfeiting, lies in its partaking of the equalizing world of cardinal numbers and their attendant abstractions.

61. Shell, loc. cit., p. 18.

62. My quotation is taken from the Riverside Edition of Emerson's *Works*, *Nature, Addresses, and Lectures*, Cambridge, Mass., 1894, pp. 35–6.

63. Ibid., pp. 36–8.

64. James, 'Emerson', reprinted in *Henry James. Selected Literary Criticism*, ed. Morris Shapira (Harmondsworth, 1968), p. 114.

65. Henry James, *The Notebooks of Henry James*, ed. F. O. Matthiessen and Kenneth Murdock (New York, 1955), pp. 12–13.

66. A random sample suggests that the most common epithets are, of course, 'fortune-hunter' and 'adventurer' (see, for example, Richard Poirier, *The Comic Sense of Henry James* (London, 1960), p. 178), usually in contexts, such as Poirier's, which include no substantial discussion of Townsend at all. The closer analyses are more specifically condemnatory. John Lucas refers to Townsend's 'coarseness' and finds him to be a 'coward' ('*Washington Square*', *The Air of Reality: New Essays on Henry James*, ed. John Goode (London, 1972), pp. 42, 55 and 56); for F. W. Dupee, he 'crudely deserts' Catherine (*Henry James* (New York, 1951), p. 64); Mary Doyle Springer locates an 'insufficiency of moral character' (*A Rhetoric of Literary Character: Some Women of Henry James* (Chicago, 1978), p. 78); Stuart Hutchinson, who is generally more sympathetic towards Townsend than most of the commentators, finds that he treats Catherine 'abominably' (*Henry James: An American as Modernist* (London and Totowa, New Jersey, 1982), p. 19); J. A. Ward sees him as 'a conniver and a scoundrel' ('Henry James's America: Versions of Oppression', *Mississippi Quarterly*, 13 (Spring 1959–60), 40); Robert R. Johannsen writes of his 'devilish charms' ('Two Sides of Washington Square', *South Carolina Review*, 7 (April 1974), 63); William Kenney regards him as 'devious and calculating' ('Dr. Sloper's Double in *Washington Square*', *The University Review—Kansas City*, 36 (Summer 1970), 301); and Millicent Bell summarizes Townsend's character as 'unnatural, unspontaneous, insincere' with 'a well-developed sense . . . of the uses of things' ('Style as Subject: *Washington Square*', *Sewanee Review*, 83 (Winter 1975), 25).

67. 'He had forgotten that in any event Catherine had her own ten thousand a year; he had devoted an abundance of meditation to this circumstance. But with his fine parts he rated himself high, and he had a perfectly definite appreciation of his value, which seemed to him inadequately represented by the sum I have mentioned' (p. 159).

68. 'Doctor Sloper's opposition was the unknown quantity in the problem he had to work out. The natural way to work it out was by marrying Catherine; but in mathematics there are many short cuts, and Morris was not without a hope that he should yet discover one' (p. 159).

69. The idea of paralysis here refers to the ways in which both science and commerce empty their objects of process understood historically, freeze them, as it were, from the ravages of nature. Such paralysis is shared by scientific law and commodities in the market.

70. John Lucas, 'Washington Square', *The Air of Reality*, ed. John Goode (London, 1972), p. 39. Cf. Richard Poirier, *The Comic Sense of Henry James* (London, 1966), p. 166.

71. Mrs. Penniman, the most explicitly theatrically inclined character in the novel, marks its extreme disablement; as an unmarried woman, she simply has no function other than to co-operate within society's determinant nexus by means of her melodramatic machinations. (This is a point usefully touched upon in Mary Doyle Springer, *A Rhetoric of Literary Character. Some Women of Henry James* (Chicago, 1978), pp. 81–5.)

72. Henry James, *Hawthorne* (1879), ed. Tony Tanner (London, 1967), p. 45.

73. There is, of course, considerable doubt as to whether he is telling the truth about his job; his evasiveness suggests that he may well be lying.

74. Norman Sidney Buck, *The Development of the Organisation of Anglo-American Trade 1800–1850* (1925; Newton Abbot, 1969), p. 16.

75. We should note in addition, however, that in his portrayal of Townsend, James is probably also making a point about the presentation of character to realign an imbalance he notes on behalf of Hawthorne's presentation in *The House of the Seven Gables*. Holgrave, in James's reading just prior to *Washington Square*, is given as 'a kind of national type'—'that of the young citizen of the United States whose fortune is simply in his lively intelligence, and who stands naked, as it were, unbiased and unencumbered alike, in the centre of the far-stretching level of American life'. James regrets the potency of Hawthorne's typology in this instance because it is simply too strong for the battle with Judge Pyncheon; a more 'lusty conservative' is needed to match the 'strenuous radical' and so, 'As it is, the mustiness and mouldiness of the tenants of the House of the Seven Gables crumble away rather too easily' (*Hawthorne*, ed. cit., p. 123).

I am not inviting a view of Sloper and Townsend as James's version of a similar clash between the old and the new which would correct the imbalance he notes in Hawthorne, but suggesting that his concern with Townsend's shadowiness might be further considered in the wider terms of the disposition of character. At the least, James's reading of Holgrave suggests possibilities for some sympathy on behalf of Townsend.

76. Barthes, 'Myth Today', loc. cit., p. 155.

77. Ibid., p. 138.

# 2

# Henry James and 'The Papers'

by DAVID HOWARD

> . . . he and his companion were alike prompted to one of those
> slightly violent returns on themselves and the work they were
> doing which none but the vulgar-minded altogether avoid.
> ('The Papers')[1]

> . . . persons not only discussing questions supposedly reserved
> for the Fates, but absolutely enacting some encounter of these
> portentous forces. ('The Papers', p. 227)

But at contact with the harsh new America, the old Balzac in
James revives. I do not know why more has not been made by
James's critics—especially by the critics of the left, who are so
certain that there is nothing in him—of his unfinished novel, *The
Ivory Tower*. The work of his all but final period has been 'poetic'
rather than 'realistic'; but now he passes into still a further
phase, in which the poetic treatment is applied to what is for
James a new kind of realism. The fiction of his latest period is
preoccupied in a curious way with the ugly, the poor, and the old,
even with—what is unprecedented for James—the grotesque. It
is perhaps the reflection of his own old age, his own lack of
worldly success, the strange creature that he himself has become.
This new vein begins I think with 'The Papers', with its
fantastically amusing picture of the sordid lives of journalists in
London. (Edmund Wilson, 'The Ambiguity of Henry James')[2]

This is one of the few interesting things said about 'The
Papers', in a brilliant essay which the critical memory has

49

confined to its opening pages on *The Turn of the Screw*. There is little else, apart from the indefatigable Gale, and the enthusiastic Gorley Putt,[3] who recommended it pleasantly and quoted it lavishly, and then had it reprinted (although in a way still hidden, inside *The Aspern Papers*). It seems typical too that Wilson gets the period slightly wrong, suggesting that the tale belongs with the later 'American period'. Similarly, it is placed in the last volume of Edel's edition of *The Collected Tales*, without explanation and without comment of any kind. It has been easy to miss.

So the first attraction it offers is that of relatively untrodden ground, and my first, indeed main proposition, is that here is a neglected fine late James long short story, written at the same time as 'The Beast in the Jungle' and 'The Birthplace'. The text is attractive in another sense: there appears to be no problem of the text, no need to enter the jungle of textual variants. 'The Papers' had no magazine publication. In 1902 when James had finished *The Wings of the Dove*, he was collecting together tales already published in magazines for a book to be called *The Better Sort*. He needed some extra stories to make up the volume. The stories he wrote in the Summer and Autumn of 1902 were 'The Beast in the Jungle', 'The Birthplace' and 'The Papers'. *The Better Sort* was published in 1903. The story was not included in the New York Edition, though of course it was in Lubbock's edition of the complete works (after James's death) and Edel's *Collected Tales*.

Like the other two new stories, it did not come out of the blue; like them its situation, the donée, had been recorded in *The Notebooks* the previous year:

> Something like the man who subscribes to an agency for 'clippings' . . . to send him everything 'that appears about him', and finds that nothing ever appears, that he never receives anything. . . . And connection between that and notion suggested by little case of woman writing to me (to fill in some paper) on behalf of *Outlook*. The case of the Newspaper girl or man who *needs* your reply, your taking *some* notice—suggesting at once the little antithesis for tale: the would-be newspaperite whom, by a *guignon*, of his, of hers, people never answer (and sadness of that); and the other who finds that they never fail, that they leap, bound at him, press, surge, scream to be

advertised; and ugliness of *that*. Awfully good little possibility seems to me to abide in it, as contrast and link between them—different shows of human egoism and the newspaper scramble: or even in the opposition, conjunction, *rencontre* of failure-girl and man first named.[4]

In the final story these are the main characters: the failure-girl is Maud Blandy (the story was going to be named after her), her more successful colleague is Howard Bight, and the seeker for publicity is Mortimer Marshal. But with a great leap of invention another character is added (although often referred to, he never actually 'appears'), Sir A. B. C. Beadel-Muffet, a man who is continually in the news, continually getting publicity without actually doing anything. Also his fiancée, a wealthy widow, Mrs. Chorner, who to begin with hates publicity (she also does not appear in person). What the final story hinges on is Beadel-Muffett's desperate attempt to escape publicity, an attempt that seems to lead to his death.

What is missing from the sketch, too, is any hint that this situation would yield a celebration of youth, or that it would yield one of the strangest, most attractive, and happiest of James's love stories, coming at the end of a volume dedicated to defeat and failure, to 'broken wings'. Of course it does state a major theme, 'different shows of human egoism and the newspaper scramble'. But, in relation to that, the most instructive thing here is that sudden rush of language in the middle—'they never fail, that they leap, bound at him, press, surge, scream to be advertised.' That anticipates the immense vigour of the language in the story itself. And of course the final version becomes much longer than 'the good little possibility' anticipated. Edel has called it 'long drawn-out',[5] but I would report an impression of concentration and economy.

To indicate some of its more obvious qualities: all that the story does is done with marvellous comic verve and invention. This is Maud reporting to Howard the rich Marshal's inclination to marry her, 'It's like making, in one of those big domestic siphons, the luxury of the poor, your own soda-water. It comes cheaper, and it's always on the side-board' (p. 174). Howard tantalizes his rival by taking him to a picturesquely cheap café and have him observe 'at the other end of the room, in the person of the little quiet man with blue spectacles and obvious wig, the greatest authority in London about the inner life of the criminal classes' (p. 195).

And like so much of late James, it is brilliantly obscene. There is a submerged identification throughout of the appetite for publicity with sexual appetite. That is planted early on when Howard Bight says 'They all do it, as the song is at the music-halls. . . . You've thought there were some high souls that didn't do it . . .' (p. 141). And this underlying reference emerges with splendid grossness in such items as the machines for stretching trousers. It is backed up by a menagerie of animal imagery and an accumulation of machine imagery too, often 'modern conveniences'. About Beadel-Muffet's failure to drop out of the news, 'The workshop of silence roars like the Zoo at dinner-time' (p. 175). Everyone is both a machine and a beast in the jungle.

Sexual exuberance connects with literary exuberance. The imagery is mock-epic:

> He *can't* disappear; he hasn't weight enough to sink; the splash the diver makes, you know, tells where he is. If you ask me what I am doing, I'm holding him under water. But we're in the middle of the pond, and the banks are thronged with spectators, and I'm expecting from day to day to see stands erected and gate-money taken. (p. 175)

We know where we quite properly are—with the dunces in Grub Street. But there is a difference. In this Grub Street, the intelligence, the wit, the imagination and the poise, comes from the hacks. The contempt is reversed.

I will draw on one more extended image in illustration of this literary exuberance in 'The Papers'. It is one of the many images that the poor Mortimer Marshal attracts. He is everything from a china plate to a gaping fish to a living-room carpet. But also sometimes something more spectacular (Maud is thinking of Howard sending up Mortimer):

> He would inflate their foolish friend with knowledge that was false and so start him as a balloon for the further gape of the world. This was the image, in turn, that would yield the last sport—the droll career of the wretched man as wandering forever through space under the apprehension, in time duly

52

gained, that the least touch of earth would involve the smash of his car. Afraid, thus, to drop, but at the same time equally out of conceit of the chill air of the upper and increasing solitudes to which he has soared, he would become such a diminishing speck, though traceably a prey to wild human gyrations, as she might conceive Bight to keep him in view for future recreation. (p. 215)

Like all truly comic sublime this has real sublime in it, with who knows what force for the turn of the century—their sense of space and cosmic isolation? But in reaching for the resonance there are certain literary names to hand, such as Jules Verne and H. G. Wells, to indicate a popular literature flourishing at this time. When interviewed, Marshal himself announces a preference for 'the novel of adventure' over the 'novel of subtlety'.

But it is not all the comic sublime. There is the extraordinary modulation into pathos and delicacy, subtle psychological adventure and discovery, in the middle section (5). Maud's baffled conciousness of the growth of her regard for Howard, her growing sense of herself as a woman, of being regarded as a woman, is too long to quote, but it is very fine. And it is one of the achievements of 'The Papers', its careful presentation of the growth of the relationship between Maud and Howard, one of the justifications for the length of the tale. The emphasis I would want to make is that this love is not (until the end perhaps) conceived as something apart from the world of the papers—intensities, absurdities, and sublimities, are made up in its terms. Thus the offering or sacrificing of self is conceived as the offer of an interview:

> 'But that was before she had killed him. Trust me, she'll chatter now.'
> This, for his companion, simply forced it out. 'It wasn't *she* who killed him. That, my dear, you know.'
> 'You mean it was I who did it? Well then, my child, interview *me*.' And, with his hands in his pockets and his idea apparently genuine, he smiled at her, by the grey river and under the high lamps, with an effect strange and suggestive. '*That* would be a go!'
> 'You mean'—she jumped at it—'you'll tell me what you know?'

'Yes, and even what I've done! But—if you'll take it so—for the Papers. Oh, for the Papers only!'

She stared. 'You mean you want me to get it in—?'

'I don't "want" you to do anything. But I'm ready to help you, ready to get it in for you, like a shot, myself, if it's a thing you yourself want.'

'A thing I want—to give you away?'

'Oh,' he laughed, 'I'm just now worth giving! You'd really do it, you know. And, to help you, here I am. It *would* be for you—only judge!—a leg up.'

It would indeed, she really saw; somehow, on the spot, she believed it. But his surrender made her tremble. It wasn't a joke—she *could* give him away; or rather she could sell him for money. Money, thus, was what he offered her, or the value of money, which was the same; it was what he wanted her to have. She was conscious already, however, that she could have it only as he offered it, and she said therefore, but half-heartedly, 'I'll keep your secret.'

He looked at her more gravely. 'Ah, as a secret I can't give it.' Then he hesitated. 'I'll get you a hundred pounds for it.'

'Why don't you,' she asked, 'get them for yourself?'

'Because I don't care for myself. I only care for you.'

She waited again. 'You mean for my taking you?' And then as he but looked at her: 'How should I take you if I had dealt with you that way?'

'What do I lose by it,' he said, 'if, by our understanding of the other day, since things have so turned out, you're not to take me at all? So, at least, on my proposal, you get something else.'

'And what,' Maud returned, 'do you get?'

'I *don't* "get"; I lose. I *have* lost. So I don't matter.' (p. 208)

The first 'she' is Mrs. Chorner who had been against publicity. Now Beadel-Muffet is apparently dead by suicide, both she and Bight can be said to have 'killed' him in that both egged him on to escape publicity. 'Kill' is one of the words of exchange in much of James, but it clearly has a special propriety in a story set in the world of newspapers. But what I would stress most is the language of commodity and money exchange: 'she could sell him for money', and the brilliantly maintained idea of the reporter as his own product.

I will now focus on three elements in the story which will briefly take me into larger Jamesian themes: the obvious one, the papers themselves, 'the newspaper scramble', the world of publicity and the figure of the journalist; a religiosity, the characteristic resort to the language and resonance of the sacred, the sacrificial, and the transcendent; and the element of bitterness and revenge, the motif of violence, of an irony and intelligence that 'kill'.

The interest in newspapers and the journalist can be found throughout James's work. He had of course been a journalist of sorts himself. One thinks of such figures as Henrietta Stackpole in *The Portrait of a Lady*, Flack in *The Reverberator*, and Morton Densher in *The Wings of the Dove*. Chad appears to be going into advertising at the end of *The Ambassadors*. Many other stories could be mobilized, but the obvious text to go to seems to be *The Bostonians*, and the obvious figure Matthias Pardon:

> All things with him referred themselves to print, and print meant simply infinite reporting, a promptitude of announce-ment, abusive when necessary, or even when not, about his fellow-citizens. He poured contumely on their private life, on their personal appearance, with the best conscience in the world. His faith, again, was the faith of Selah Tarrant—that being in the newspapers is a condition of bliss, and that it would be fastidious to question the terms of the privilege ... a thoroughly modern young man; he had no idea of not taking advantage of all the modern conveniences. He regarded the mission of mankind upon earth as a perpetual evolution of telegrams; everything to him was very much the same, he had no sense of proportion or quality; but the newest thing was what came nearest exciting in his mind the sentiment of respect.[6]

For him, again like Selah Tarrant, 'human existence was a huge publicity'.

Now this would seem to give us a firm, energetic, satirical stance on the papers, a stance that informs all of James's attention to them, making him a commentator on the well-known phenomenon of their 'rise', particularly the cheap daily press (James stresses that 'the papers' involved in the story are 'Daily'), in America and Britain in the late nineteenth and early twentieth centuries. They exhibit the commercial vulgarity of modern civilization, the corruption of the truth and the word, the loss of value and discrimination. By the time of 'The Papers' the increase and expansion of the press was even greater, with the added factor of newspaper empires like those of Northcliff and Hearst, and the increasing stress on advertising.[7]

The theme, especially in its extension as the theme of publicity—'the laws so mysterious, so curious, so interesting—that govern the great currents of public attention'—is very much present in other of James's late work. This is part of Longden's introduction to the new world of London (the motif of exposure will later include the flesh of Tishy Grenden at her shocking party):

> She has in her expression all that's charming in her nature. But, beauty, in London, staring, glaring, obvious, knock-down, beauty, as plain as a poster on a wall, an advertisement of soap or whiskey, something that speaks to the crowd and crosses the footlights, fetches such a price in the market, that the absence of it, for a woman with a girl to marry, inspires endless terror and constitutes for the wretched pair—to speak of mother and daughter alone—a sort of social bankruptcy. London doesn't love the latent or the lurking, has neither time, nor taste, nor sense for anything less discernible than the red flag in front of the steam-roller. It wants cash over the counter and letters ten feet high.[8]

The security of this theme could again be confirmed by the other stories in *The Better Sort*. Setting aside what many would consider to be the masterpiece of the volume, 'The Beast in the Jungle', they add up to a panorama of the vulgarity and commercialism of the age, in which innocence, sensitivity, and intelligence inevitably suffer, in which, to draw on James's own resonant use of idiom, everyone and everything are *sold*. 'We live in an age of prodigious machinery, all organized to a single end. That end is publicity' ('Flickerbridge').[9] These stories are full of sensitive gentlemen and women who reluctantly serve, exist by serving, a crass civilization, who are themselves commodities or produce commodities. In 'Broken Wings' writer and artist agree that they have 'imagination' which is 'an article we have to supply'.[10] The curator of 'The

Birthplace', compelled into a vulgar routine of the presentation of Shakespeare, to meet public demand, cries 'They kill
HIM every day.'[11] These people are the real better sort.

And they include the journalists in 'The Papers'. They are
two poor sensitives who have become disgusted with their part
in the world of publicity, disgusted with the papers themselves, the public they serve, and the 'better sort' like
Mortimer Marshal and Beadel-Muffet who seek through
them to become public figures, and disgusted with the effect
their job has on themselves. 'It makes one cruel . . . our trade
does' (p. 146). They decide to 'chuck in the papers'.

But it is obvious from this that if there is a security of
satirical stance toward the world of publicity, the journalist is
not the object of the satire as seemed to be the case with
Pardon in *The Bostonians*. One of the fascinations about the
rather clogged opening pages of 'The Papers' is that James
seems to be working off a similar savage treatment of Blandy
and Bight, before developing an intricate sympathy for them
in the body of the story. The main object of satire switches to
the people that appear or desire to appear in the papers,
particularly the better sort, the people that is who would
appear to be the victims of the press in that passage from *The
Bostonians*. It is Beadel-Muffet who exploits Bight. It is Bight
who in his attempted 'plotting' against Beadel-Muffet gets the
increasing sense 'of having been sold again'.

In this way, as I have suggested, the journalists join the
ranks in the stories of this period of the proletariate of the
imagination, the denizens of the new Grub Street (they move
on into plays and tales). Gissing is an obvious figure to invoke
here because of his sympathy for and horror at the intellectual
proletariate of his *New Grub Street*, and also because James
knew him and admired the novel. In a period in which many
writers began as journalists, such as Arnold Bennett and
Theodore Dreiser, James knew many who had been or still
were journalists: H. G. Wells, Stephen Crane, Harold Frederic,
for example.

There is then a ready context, a context involving an
awareness of the contemporary literary market, for James's
sympathy in 'The Papers'. Critics with a habit of snobbery
towards journalism may too easily draw on the definite disposal

of Matthias Pardon, as they can draw on the later quarrel with Wells, 'I had rather be called a journalist than an artist, that is the essence of it, and there was no other antagonist possible than yourself',[12] to set up, with James at the forefront, the battle of art against journalism. In the matter of the figure of the journalist at least, the matter is more complicated.

But to take this point further: I have argued elsewhere[13] that the secure satirical stance of *The Bostonians*, its apparent disgust at the American scene, is endlessly qualified by a lyrical generosity, particularly through the figure of Verena Tarrant. So that what on the one hand seems to be firmly placed—for example the remark about Pardon that 'everything to him was very much the same'—can reappear elsewhere as something positive and vital, as an animating principle. So that apart from the figure of the journalist, what ought to be more in doubt too is this discriminating vision of the vulgar world of publicity.

What else attaches to the notion of publicity in James? We have touched briefly on the perceived threat to the values of privacy and integrity, the vulgarization of society, the exhibition of a blatantly commercial social system. There is, especially in 'The Papers', a contempt for a society based on advertising (crucial to the expansion of the daily press) and for a society based on the conspicuous consumption of the better sort (the leisure class)—Maud envies and is disgusted by Marshal's modern appliances (knowing that she might become one of them).

But there is something more than the personal and social here; we seem to be in, however playfully, metaphysical territory, where existence *is* a publicity. To live is to be published, to have come out, to have appeared. 'Do let me happen!' pleads Mortimer Marshal.

It would be worthwhile recalling in this context that 'The Beast in the Jungle' is about a man, 'the man of his time, *the* man, to whom nothing on earth was to have happened'.[14] We read it conventionally as the story of a man who misses out on life, who in his obsession with 'being kept for something rare and strange' learns too late the value of love and the horror of egotism. And certainly one would want to use the story to throw into relief the affirmation of human love in 'The Papers'. But as well as a moral concern, 'The Beast in the Jungle' has a power to do with a metaphysical urgency, an ontological obsession. It is less that March is to blame, more that he is the man not allowed to happen.

I want to locate this element in 'The Papers' with a quotation which will also include the religiose (Mortimer Marshal has been seeking the aid of the journalists to take Beadel-Muffet's place):

'I've ventured,' Mr. Marshal glowed back, 'to come and remind you that the hours are fleeting.'

Bight had surveyed him with eyes perhaps equivocal. 'You're afraid someone else will step in?'

'Well, with the place so tempting and so empty—!'

Maud made herself again his voice. 'Mr. Marshal sees it empty itself perhaps too fast.'

He acknowledged, in his large, bright way, the help afforded him by her easy lightness. 'I do want to get in, you know, before anything happens.'

'And what,' Bight inquired, 'are you afraid *may* happen?'

'Well, to make sure,' he smiled, 'I want myself, don't you see, to happen first.'

Our young woman, at this, fairly fell, for her friend, into his sweetness. '*Do* let him happen!'

'*Do* let me happen!' Mr. Marshal followed it up.

They stood there together, where they had paused, in their strange council of three, and their extraordinary tone, in connection with their number, might have marked them, for some passer catching it, as persons not only discussing questions supposedly reserved for the Fates, but absolutely enacting some encounter of these portentous forces. 'Let you—let you?' Bight gravely echoed, while on the sound, for the moment, immensities might have hung. It was as far, however, as he was to have time to speak, for even while his voice was in the air another, at first remote and vague, joined it there on an ominous note and hushed all else to stillness. It came, through the roar of thoroughfares, from the direction of Fleet Street, and it made our interlocutors exchange an altered look. They recognised it, the next thing, as the howl, again of the Strand, and then but an instant elapsed before it flared into the night. 'Return of Beadel-Muffet! Tremenjous Sensation!'

Tremenjous indeed, so tremenjous that, each really turning as pale with it as they had turned, on the same spot, the other time and with the other news, they stood long enough striken and still for the cry, multiplied in a flash, again to reach them. They couldn't have said afterwards who first took it up. 'Return—?'

'From the *Dead*—I *say!*' poor Marshal piercingly quavered.

'Then he *hasn't* been—?' Maud gasped it with him at Bight.

But that genius, clearly, was not less deeply affected. 'He's alive?', he breathed in a long, soft wail in which admiration appeared at first to contend with amazement and then the sense of the comic to triumph over both. Howard Bight uncontrollably—it might have struck them as almost hysterically—laughed.

The others could indeed but stare. 'Then who's dead?' piped Mortimer Marshal.

'I'm afraid Mr. Marshal that *you* are,' the young man returned, more gravely, after a minute. He spoke as if he saw *how* dead. (p. 226)

This is splendidly and playfully profound. One notes the touches of late Shakespeare: he that was lost is found. And that itself is part of this vocabulary of fate, creation, sacrifice, transcendence, immortality. We are attending a miracle, a rebirth. The Christian level of reference is confirmed by Maud a little later in the same scene, 'To have given it all up, and yet to have it all . . . to have more than all.'

The incident in late James of the transcendent is a rich and complicated area, and here I do little more than to add to the list, to the varieties of religious experience, in the late work, to ponder at (he had read his brother's book). There are many ways of treating this element, and the treatments involve a fascinating cluster of names: Swedenborg, Henry James Senior, William James, Walter Pater, Maurice Maeterlinck, and perhaps D'Annunzio, on whom James had written a long critical essay at this time. But the perspective I am most interested in using is that developed by John Goode in his chapter on *The Wings of the Dove* in *The Air of Reality*.

This entertains the proposition that James is engaged in an elaborate account (and possibly defence) of a civilization based on exploitation and the accumulation of great wealth in a few hands, through an enactment in his fiction of a series of renunciations, of symbolic givings up, which justify actual possession. Envy and resentment are warded off by the spectacle of sacrifice, or the exhibition of transcendent values;

they become transformed into an acceptance by the dispossessed of their real renunciation. One implication of this is
that these 'renunciations' are the highest luxury of a leisure
class, their most conspicuous consumptions, something only
they can afford—death, in Venice. This is what Milly Theale
in *The Wings of the Dove* dies of: conspicuous consumption. And
for this display, publicity, whether art or the papers, is
essential. This is where the artist and the intellectual are sold
and sell, where they produce.

Beadel-Muffet then, in 'The Papers', does not simply
represent the appetite for publicity of his class, he represents
the conquest by that class of transcendental space and
discourse. As the two journalists wryly agree at the end, he is
now immortal. But the actual effect of this, and the other
transcendental references I have drawn on—giving up all,
wanting to happen—is clearly one of comic extravagance,
similar in tone to the bizarre extended images. In this story the
transcendental elements create not mystery but absurdity, and
throw into relief its ironic human centre—Maud and
Howard—and their discovery of their love. Mysteries are sent
up in favour of the 'mystery' of the other.

The sceptical account I briefly drew on of the religious and
metaphysical presence in later James, then, is borne out by
'The Papers'. Of course Beadel-Muffet and Mortimer Marshal
are clearer cases than Milly Theale or Maggie Verver. Yet with
'The Papers' in mind it might be easier to read those figures and
their novels as sardonic types of the better sort.

But there is one more thing to say. Beyond the quiet
affirmation of unpublished love and the exuberant representation of a decadent society, there is this presence of resentment
and revenge. I have already noticed this in a general way by
connecting the journalists with the other dispossessed figures in
the stories of this period. They are part of 'that community of
fatigue and failure and, after all, intelligence' which is conscious
that 'isn't it only we who do pay'[15] ('Mrs. Medwin'), that they
are 'helping to hold it up'[16] ('Broken Wings'). Maud Blandy
envies the wealth of Mortimer Marshal, but it is Howard Bight
whose resentment is strongest, in his savage contempt for
Beadel-Muffet and Marshal, and his consciousness of being
used:

with the life we lead and the age we live in, there's always something the matter with me—there can't help being: some rage, some disgust, some fresh amazement against which one hasn't, for all one's experience, been proof. That sense— of having been sold again. (p. 191)

We may say that exactly what the love story involves is this bitterness in Howard being offset by a growing capacity for pity in Maud, a growing tenderness which is partly put in terms of her transition from bachelor girl, looking like a man, to woman. She 'saves' him. It's part of saving him from the cruelty of his trade. But we have to recognize too that Maud is attracted by the cruelty in Howard, despite her decision that she won't marry him if he has hounded Beadel-Muffet to his death. There is more than one kind of love:

> Yes, it was life again, bitter, doubtless, but with a taste, when, having stopped her cab, short of her indication, in Covent Garden, she walked across southward and to the top of the street in which she and her friend had last parted with Mortimer Marshal. She came down to their favoured pothouse, the scene of Bight's high compact with that worthy, and here, hesitating, she paused, uncertain as to where she had best look out. Her conviction, on her way, had but grown; Howard Bight would be looking out—*that* to a certainty; something more, something portentous, had happened (by her evening paper, scanned in the light of her little shop window, she had taken instant possession of it), and this would have made him know that she couldn't keep up what he would naturally call her 'game'. There were places where they often met, and the diversity of these—not too far apart, however—would be his only difficulty. He was on the prowl, in fine, with his hat over his eyes; and she hadn't known, till this vision of him came, what seeds of romance were in her soul. Romance, the other night, by the river, had brushed them with a wing that was like the blind bump of a bat, but that had been something on his part, whereas this thought of bringing him succour as to a Russian anarchist, to some victim of society or subject of extradition, was all her own, and was of this special moment. She *saw* him with his hat over his eyes; she saw him with his overcoat collar turned up; she saw him as a hunted hero cleverly drawn in one of the serialising weeklies, or, as they said, in some popular 'ply', and the effect of it was to open to her on the spot a sort of

happy sense of all her possible immorality. That was the romantic sense, and everything vanished but the richness of her thrill. She knew little enough what she might have to do for him, but her hope, as sharp as a pang, was that, if anything, it would put her in danger too. The hope, as it happened then, was crowned on the very spot; she had never felt so in danger as when, just now, turning to the glazed door of the cookshop, she saw a man, within, close behind the glass, still, stiff, and ominous, looking at her hard. The light of the place was behind him, so that his face, in the dusk of the side-street, was dark, but it was visible that she showed for him as an object of interest. The next thing, of course, she had seen more—seen she could be such an object, in such a degree, only to her friend himself, and that Bight had thus been sure of her; and the next thing after that had passed straight in and been met by him, as he stepped aside to admit her, in silence. He *had* his hat pulled down and, quite forgetfully, in spite of the warmth within, the collar of his mackintosh up. (p. 217)

Now of course this is offered comically and luridly, the romance of the victim and the dispossessed. Howard as the hunted murderer of Beadel-Muffet is absurd. Maud's thrill at her possible danger is deflated when the man gazing so hard at her turns out to be Howard: 'she could be such an object [of interest] . . . only to her friend himself', with another implication that she is really in danger from him. But I feel there is more to this than fantasy or the absurd. There is a sense not that Howard did murder Beadel-Muffet but that he might have done or should have done. It is also an expression, only partly ironic, of her love and resentment, that is to say, it is a contemplation however indirect of actual life and death, of actual challenge and victimization. And it competes with the transcendent. It is a register of her irony and intelligence which is not reduced to diffidence. She knows she is thinking in terms of weekly serials and popular plays. But that doesn't prevent her so thinking. The point is not that she has been corrupted by cheap literature. It may be that the energies it carries are not available in the better sort of literature. It may be that they are going on to write such tales and plays, not simply about Russian anarchists and victims of society on the run, but as direct challenges to that society.

NOTES

1. *The Aspern Papers and Other Stories* (Penguin Modern Classics, 1976), p. 141. For convenience all references to 'The Papers' will be to this edition. Reference to the other stories that were published with 'The Papers' will be to the first edition of *The Better Sort*.
2. *The Triple Thinkers* (Pelican, 1962), p. 137.
3. Robert L. Gale, *Plots and Characters in the Fiction of Henry James* (Archon, 1965), and S. Gorley Putt, *The Fiction of Henry James: A Readers' Guide* (Penguin, 1968).
4. *The Notebooks of Henry James*, ed. F. O. Matthiessen and Kenneth B. Murdock (Oxford, 1947), p. 313.
5. Leon Edel, *The Life of Henry James*, Vol. 2 (Penguin, 1977), p. 473.
6. *The Bostonians* (Penguin Modern Classics, 1966), p. 107.
7. Still one of the best short accounts of the press in this period is in Raymond Williams, *The Long Revolution* (Pelican, 1965).
8. *The Awkward Age* (Penguin Modern Classic, 1966), p. 42.
9. *The Better Sort* (Methuen, 1903), p. 121.
10. *The Better Sort*, p. 16.
11. *The Better Sort*, p. 207.
12. *Henry James and H. G. Wells*, ed. Leon Edel and Gordon N. Ray (Rupert Hart-Davies, 1958), p. 264.
13. '*The Bostonians*', *The Air of Reality: New Essays on Henry James*, ed. John Goode (Methuen, 1972), pp. 60–80.
14. *The Better Sort*, p. 178.
15. *The Better Sort*, p. 88.
16. *The Better Sort*, p. 2.

# 3

# *The Turn of the Screw* and the *Recherche de L'Absolu*

by MILLICENT BELL

The preoccupation of a generation of critics with the reality status of the ghosts in Henry James's *The Turn of the Screw* has always seemed to me misplaced. One may grant that the spectral appearances to which the governess in the tale testifies cannot be proven to be supernaturally actual or her illusion, that we are in a condition of uncertainty over the question and that the story merits the title of 'fantastic' which Todorov gives it. But is this not a minor source of our interest? The reader's epistemological quandary, his inability to be positive about how to 'take' the phenomena reported by the narrator is, of course, rooted in his inability to verify or refute her first-person account; we cannot escape the enclosure of her mind, and all efforts to find internal clues of veracity or distortion in what she tells us are baffled by its essential mode. The confidence she has inspired in her fictional editor, Douglas, does not really help, either, for he, too, is a possibly compromised and implicated speaker over whose shoulder the first-person narrator of the frame-story looks at us without either reassurance or scepticism. But her report perplexes the reader in other ways too; the principle of uncertainty operates more fundamentally in leaving us in doubt about her way of reading experience generally, her evaluation of herself and others, her identification of motive and meaning in their behaviour and her own, her moral vision. One may say that the presence or absence of the Miss Jessel and Peter Quint at Bly is crucial in such a judgement; if they are to be believed in, she is justified in her view of the children and her sense of her own duty, and if not, she is a victim of delusion. But, in fact, this is not so. Though the story gains its special *frisson* from its fantastic element, one can conceive an equally powerful Jamesian mystery that might be based entirely on the moral uncertainty alone. One has only to think of another work, *The Sacred Fount*, to see that James could have composed a fiction whose indeterminacy is rooted in our unease concerning the narrator's deductions and judgements about others, his purely visual perceptions being never in doubt.

Todorov has himself noticed that in some of James's ghost stories the quality of the fantastic is threatened by the possibility of allegory. In 'The Private Life', the double who sits at his desk writing while another self occupies himself with mundanity may or may not be a supernatural presence, but he is so much more obviously a symbolic figure in a fable of the artist's nature that the hesitation of the fantastic is almost eliminated. He finds *The Turn of the Screw*, on the other hand, James's most realized example of the fantastic, one that maintains its uncertainty throughout the text and keeps it to the forefront. But I would argue that it, too, is a fable. And I would support this view by means of another insight of Todorov which he does not apply closely to *The Turn of the Screw*—that many of James's fictions concern themselves with the act of perception turned towards an absence, that they are quest stories in which the pursuit of some phantasmal object without presence except to the perceiver threatens the ambivalence of the fantastic, makes meaningless the question, 'Does the ghost exist?' Precisely this happens, I think, in *The Turn of the Screw*. The story, I would urge further, represents a search for an absence that is not restrictedly 'ghostly'. It is not the ghost of the two dead household servants that the governess seeks to validate, but something more undenotable, an evil in the children and in the world which the ghosts can be said simply to represent. This absence can never be converted to presence; precisely for that reason all reader curiosity about the children's relation with the dead or proofs of their corruption must be frustrated.

James would seem to have deprecated any attempt—such as this one—to take his tale very seriously, tending to reply to questions about its meaning with the evasive declaration (to H. G. Wells in 1898) that 'the thing is essentially a pot boiler.' He could still refer to it in the preface to his revision in the New York Edition as 'a piece of ingenuity pure and simple, or cold artistic calculation, an amusette to catch those not easily caught'. But what trap is laid for the over-clever may, after all, be precisely illustrated by the way puzzlement over the ghost-liness of the ghosts has led so many astray. His other remarks in this same preface are worth examining, and suggest that by calling his work one of pure ingenuity he may have meant that he had dispensed with any claim to the realistic. What he has written, after all, he tells us, was something in the mode of romance, 'a perfect example of the imagination unassisted . . . unassociated, a fairy-tale pure and simple . . . an annexed but independent world.'

But if the ghosts in *The Turn of the Screw* belong to the realm of romantic dream rather than to literal reality this does not mean that they are the dreams of a sick young woman who has hallucinated. Their irreality functions mythically, to create a profound perception about the structures of human experi-ence. Leon Edel, perhaps taking a hint from the preface, has noted the connection with the two fairy-tales James particu-larly mentions. Like Cinderella, the governess is the youngest child who ventures alone into the world dreaming of a meeting with Prince Charming. And Bluebeard's last wife, Fatima, is given the keys to the treasures and told not to enter a forbidden room. But her curiosity overcomes her and she finds the bloody corpses of her predecessors as, indeed, the governess, longing for her absent master, comes upon *her* dead predecessor. What such archetypal narratives may mean as representations of human desire and fear should concern us even in James's transforming context. He saw his governess's visions, the putative evil spirits, the demons of fairy tale, as having a symbolic function: 'They would be agents, in fact; there would be laid on them the dire duty of causing the situation to reek with the air of Evil.' By their capacity for, as it is said in the story, 'everything', by the material absence of that capitalized absolute, they would suggest a general vision which he was sure the reader could make present sufficiently out of his own memories.

But Romance is essentially Manichean. It sees the world in terms of opposed purities, allowing only for ideal virtue and undiluted viciousness, for heroes and heroines, villains and villainesses diametrically opposed, for evil and good in so complete a state that no experience we recall can fully express them. The condition of romance depends upon absence (as realism does upon presence) not because romantic narratives do not contain details but because the details are never *enough*; no amount of them will ever fill the void of the absolute, supply enough wicked deeds to justify the Wicked King's title, describe the Good Prince so that his goodness is fully accounted for. Implicit in the diametrics of the romance is the mythos of the Christian tradition which, while according responsibility for creation to one sacred being, yet suggests that God's contest with Satan splits the universe into domains of equal power, inexhaustible sources of the divine and the demonic.

In *The Turn of the Screw* this version of life is the governess's private one; she is the writer of romance, the absolutist of the Manichean interpretation of the Christian tradition. In a way, therefore, our interest in her must after all, be psychological—not in the sense of Edmund Wilson and his followers so that we may discover the cause of her hallucinations in erotic tensions but so that we may find the story's subject in her theory of experience. James's chosen technical method, the first-person narrative unillumined by exterior comment, focuses us upon her mind and its schemes of judgement. James had remarked of the ghost story generally—in another preface in the New York Edition—that

> the moving accident, the rare conjunction, whatever it be, doesn't make the story,—in the sense that the story is our excitement, our amusement, our thrill and our suspense; the human emotion and the human condition, the clustering human conditions we expect presented, only make it.

James seems to have realized only as he wrote that the story's subject was the governess's mind. He had begun with a different focus, the idea of the effect on the children of *their* sight of the apparitions, as his notebook germ, the story told him by the Archbishop of Canterbury shows. In this notation there is no hint of the narrator James would create; the Archbishop had related that he had been told about the haunted children by 'a lady who had no art of relation, and no clearness'. This original focus on the children's perceptions is preserved in the prologue of the story when Douglas speaks of the interest his tale will offer:

> I agree—in regard to Griffin's ghost, or whatever it was—that its appearing first to the little boy, at so tender an age, adds a particular touch. . . . But if the child gives the effect another turn of the screw, what do you say to *two* children—?

But, in fact, the screw of childish perception of horror is never really turned at all in the story we subsequently receive. We never witness as dramatized mental events the appearance of Quint and Miss Jessel to Flora and Miles; indeed, this gap in the presentation is so marked that there are grounds for supposing that the children never see them at all, even though the governess thinks otherwise. Instead, characteristically, James has given us still another of his studies of a consciousness intellectually and emotionally mature and refined enough to provide drama and theme. It may not be accidental that James chose to include *The Turn of the Screw* not with some of his other ghost-stories but in the volume of the New York Edition that contains *The Aspern Papers*, in which the narrator's self-presentation is the subject we are called upon to grasp and evaluate.

That the governess's mind was the story's subject Virginia Woolf perceived in 1918 when she remarked in the course of reviewing a book about the supernatural that the ghosts

> have neither the substance nor the independent existence of ghosts. The governess is not so much frightened of them as of the sudden extension of her field of perception, which in this case widens to reveal to her the presence all about her of an unmentionable evil. The appearance of the figures is an illustration, not in itself specially alarming, of a state of mind which is profoundly mysterious and terrifying.

As Woolf points out, the appearance of the figures, the onset of the 'state of mind' which is suddenly opened up to the unknown in itself, is preceded 'not by the storms and howlings of the old romances, but by an absolute hush and lapse of nature which we feel to represent the ominous trance of her own mind'. One remembers, at Woolf's reminder, the wonderful sentence in the story, 'The rooks stopped cawing in the golden sky, and the friendly evening hour lost for the unspeakable minute all its voice', which precedes the first appearance of Quint. The world of nature and the self, 'golden' and 'friendly' as Bly appears, is about to reveal itself as deceptive and corrupt.

Deceptive and corrupt, however, to a particular way of seeing. 'Seeing' is more than a matter of the eyes and the truthful record of what they register. The governess's 'seeing'—moral and metaphysical—is what we are made, by the devices of the story, to ponder, to question. James remarks in his preface that the record the governess keeps is 'crystalline', but he adds, 'by which I don't of course mean her explanation of them, a different matter'. If she is an 'unreliable narrator' it is on the grounds of judgement. If the governess sees always with an imagination that shifts alternately from a view of Bly as paradise unfallen to a view of it as permeated with corruption, it is because her mind is like one of those designs which allow us to see a flock of white birds crossing a black sky from left to right or a flock of black birds crossing a white sky from right to left—but never both flocks at once. It is an imagination incapable of perceiving ambiguity, only capable of admitting one view and excluding the other. It cannot reconcile and combine, can only exchange the view for its exclusive opposite.

Maybe this accounts for the fact that the characters' configuration in the story the governess tells consists of doubled pairs representing alternate versions of the same reality with the exception of Mrs. Grose, whose simple, whose admirable 'grossness' makes such a division impossible. The governess sees herself duplicated twice, in opposite ways, in the person of Miss Jessel and little Flora. She sees the master, whose masculine actuality is represented in her imagination as a figure either of infinite grace or infinite corruption as both little Miles and Quint.

For who is Quint in this drama of the self's revelation to itself? He is, of course, a version or inversion of the owner of

Bly, the God-like fine gentleman who has sent the governess upon her mission there with the injunction never to appeal to him—and who has caused her to fall in love with him. The governess has already admitted to Mrs. Grose that she was 'carried away in London', and the housekeeper says, 'Well, Miss, you're not the first—and you won't be the last.' The master's sexual magnetism has exercised itself—for good or evil—before, and is, in fact, soon confused with Quint's in the conversation that ensues when the governess inquires about her predecessor. That predecessor, moreover, is also a projection from within the governess—this time, of her own capacity for sexual subjection. 'She was young and pretty—almost as young and almost as pretty, Miss, even as you', says Mrs. Grose. 'He seems to like us young and pretty', says the governess, to which the answer of Mrs. Grose, is, 'Oh, he *did* . . . I means that's *his* way—the master's.' Her seeming to correct herself in this curious fashion suggests to the governess that the housekeeper is speaking of someone else. Indeed, she may be, for Quint, who is the master's 'man', also 'liked [them] young and pretty', it is soon made clear to us. On the other hand, the housekeeper may not really be referring to anyone but the master. It is only the governess who must divide the master from a double who has his capacity for vice, or from that rôle in relation to women which arouses her resentment.

It is after this conversation that the objectified image of the master as an object of hatred rather than love appears just when she has been half-expecting to meet the gentleman from Harley Street. She thinks—with one side of her mind, one might say—that he will suddenly appear, smiling and approving of her handling of the problem presented by the letter from Miles's school—the letter that suggests to her that the perfect little boy has committed some unmentionable wickedness. She has, of course, decided to do nothing—unwilling to establish the nature of the child's offence or to clear him of fault, as she could do by writing the school an inquiry. She thus retains her capacity for alternate visions of Miles who, as I have said, is also a representative of the master. And now the master's double appears in his place, an apparition whose description at first is only that he wears no

71

hat—and so is *not* a gentleman—but otherwise might be the master or the master in ungentlemanly aspect, for he wears his 'better's' clothes and 'looks like an actor', that is, an impersonation of someone else.

Quint is her intuition, then, of the evil in the fine gentleman, the benevolent masculine authority who has commanded and possessed her erotic fancy, or a version of the master as her suspicion and resentment conceive him now, at a moment of trouble when he cannot be appealed to. Miss Jessel, as I have already stated, is herself. The predecessor is seen later in postures that the governess even recognizes as her own. When she is about to write a letter to the master she is confronted by sight of this figure at her own desk, occupied in writing 'like some housemaid writing to her sweetheart'. The governess has collapsed at the foot of the steps in the lonely house after her return from her conversation with Miles outside the church— a conversation in which he tells her definitely that he must leave. She realizes that it is exactly there, identically bowed, that she has seen 'the spectre of the most horrible of women'. Her own emotions, at this moment, are those of guilt and shame—she has deserved Miles's reproach that he is kept from school and 'his own sort' by her possessive surveillance. And, perhaps, in the figure of despair, the haggard and terrible Miss Jessel, she sees the self within her which could deserve to be cast off by the master. But she cannot see herself as, in a mingled human way, both of these at the same time.

Her attachment to Miles is, by this same division of mind, also a representation of her attachment to the master. The 10-year-old boy is a 'little gentleman', an exquisite, tiny representation of male glamour, dressed, like Quint, if not in the master's clothes, at least by the master's tailor. If he is an unfallen child, an avatar of the good master, he is also Quint from whom he acquired the wickedness of adult masculinity. He has become a nephew also of Quint who as a sort of surrogate uncle, ruled the household in the master's stead, making 'too free' with the maids and with 'everyone', as Mrs. Grose remembers. To the governess, Miles is beguilingly graceful and gallant; he calls her 'my dear', he makes love to her with his flattery of her as a 'jolly perfect lady', and in the scene after Flora's departure when they dine together alone, the governess herself thinks of them as a pair of newlyweds, too shy to speak before the waiter. Indeed, she has been utterly 'carried away', just as Mrs. Grose predicted when she said, 'You will be carried away by the little gentleman', words that echo the statement that the governess had already been carried away in Harley Street. Critics have observed that the governess fastens her sexual passion, frustrated of its object in the master, upon the child, but it should be noted that Miles has enacted for his own part the master's seduction. And as its sequel, he will abandon her, by his resolution to go back to school. This is such an abandonment as she knows, the poor governess, she might expect from the master—who would also want to go back to his 'own sort', his own class. Miss Jessel, one takes it, was used and abandoned if not by the master *in proprie persona* then by his alternate, Quint.

Flora, of course, completes the symmetry of the three couples—the governess and the master, Miss Jessel and Quint, and the two children—and though there is no sexual relation between the children to make for exact duplication, she, too, stands in a slighter way for the governess. In her original beauty and innocence she is an absolute of the governess's own goodness more perfect because pre-sexual, unfallen. She, too, would be abandoned by Miles who wants to leave for his 'own sort', this time the world of masculinity from which she is divided, as a girl, as absolutely as the governess is divided from the master's and Miles's world by both class and sex. In the end, her beauty becomes suddenly ugly, hard, like Miss Jessel's, when she seems 'an old, old woman' to the governess who has, herself, by this time, lost her own innocence forever.

I have elaborated the pattern of duplicates in the story to emphasize its structure of mirroring and reversal. One can seem to say almost the same thing as I have been doing by identifying all these paired figures, or at least Miss Jessel and Quint, as hallucinatory projections of the governess's repressions. But this is to literalize the poetic design of James's fable, and to diminish its thematic strength. That design and import is rather, as I have said, the vision of a world divided, bifurcated, just as the paired figures are, into absolutes of good and evil. If such perfection of beauty, goodness, grace as represented by the

73

children exists in the world, then the opposite of these qualities is implied by them. The governess's own nature is an exhibition of a love that is hate, trust that is fear, solicitude that is destructiveness. I believe that James wishes to suggest a criticism of this view of human nature and the world at large. In this moral fable the governess's tragic fall from the rôle she imagines for herself—saviour and protector, agency of absolute goodness—brings her to that opposite condition which is conjured also by her imagination, that of destroyer. In her demand that the children admit that they have known and seen the ghosts, she is demanding their admission of their own absolute evil which must simultaneously exist as an alternative to the absolute good she has seen in them. She will not believe in Miles's attempt to convince her that he can be ordinarily bad. Believing in his absolute goodness she insists upon his capacity for some inconceivable demonstration of damnation.

A close reading of the entire story will show how its ambiguity, so often referred to, is really a kind of binary permutation in which alternatives maintain their exclusiveness. The governess's narrative language reinforces at every point the effect of a viewpoint in which assertions can be read backwards, so to speak, to mean their opposites. Such effects can be summarized in the governess's own phrase when she starts her tale: 'I remember the whole beginning as a succession of flights and drops, a little see-saw of the right throbs and the wrong.' The see-saw rhythm is immediately initiated. She had, she tells us, somehow dreaded her arrival at Bly, but was, instead, delighted by its beauty—the 'bright' flowers, the 'golden' sky—and she is received 'as if I had been the mistress', a fulfilment, seemingly, of her dream of marriage to the master. On this first evening she meets the beautiful, perfectly named Flora, and goes to bed in a grand room. But there is a 'drop' in Mrs. Grose's eagerness to see her, an excessive eagerness that implies another reading of appearances. And appearances are just what the governess will not ever trust, since all things may be replaced by their opposites.

Even when she seems to assert that things are wholly what they seem, doubt invades her sentences and makes them mean another thing entirely:

74

But it was a comfort that there could be no uneasiness in a connection with anything as beatific as the radiant image of my little girl, the vision of whose angelic beauty had probably more than anything to do with the restlessness that, before morning, made me several times rise and wander about the room to take in the whole picture and prospect, to watch from my open window the faint summer dawn, to look at such stretches of the rest of the house as I could catch, and to listen, while in the falling dusk the first birds began to twitter, for the possible recurrence of a sound or two less natural and not without but within, that I had fancied I heard.

There could be no uneasiness—yet uneasiness is precisely what the image of Flora, described in Edenic terms, provokes in her. And, not surprisingly, she soon hears, she believes, 'the cry of a child' sometime during the night. These 'fancies' were thrown off, she adds immediately, yet she contradicts their identification as fancies by promptly going on to say that 'in the light, or the gloom, I should rather say, of other and subsequent matters' these impressions would return. Examining her feelings the next morning, she produces a statement which, denying, seems to assert a ground for fear:

> What I felt the next day was, I suppose, nothing that could be fairly called a reaction from the cheer of my arrival; it was at the most only a slight oppression produced by a fuller measure of the scale, as I walked round them, gazed up at them, took them in, of my new circumstances.

As little Flora conducts her from one part of the house to another she rocks from one attitude to another:

> I had the view of a castle of romance inhabited by a rosy sprite, such a place as would somehow, for diversion of the young idea, take all colour out of story-books and fairy-tales. Wasn't it just a story-book over which I had fallen a-doze and a-dream? No; it was a big ugly antique but convenient house, embodying a few features of a building still older, half-displaced and half-utilized, in which I had the fancy of our being almost as lost as a handful of passengers in a great drifting ship.

And so the first little chapter ends, and the next begins with a 'this' whose referent is, presumably, this second view of Bly which is said to have come home to her when she went to meet 'the little gentleman' and during the evening was 'deeply disconcerted' by the letter which arrives from Miles's school. She does not read it to Mrs. Grose but she admits that it says only that he cannot be kept on, which immediately means to her 'that he's an injury to others'. She asks Mrs. Grose if she has ever known the boy to be bad, to which the housekeeper, who does not think in absolutes, as I have said, eagerly assents, while vigorously rejecting the terms the governess employs—'contaminate', 'corrupt'—in reference to him. As I have already noted, however, the governess will never really be convinced, even by Miles himself, that he is capable of venial fault, only, as he is angelic, of demonic wickedness, like Satan himself for whom there could have been no half-way halting-place between Heaven and the Hell to which he fell. So she continues to invoke by denial a wicked Miles. After meeting him, she is ready to pronounce it 'monstrous' she says, that 'such a child as had now been revealed to me should be under an interdict'. And her sentences still continue their curious game: 'It would have been impossible to carry a bad name with a greater sweetness of innocence.'

It becomes structurally necessary, as the story advances, that this see-saw play be kept up, that the choice between the alternatives be put off as long as possible. So the governess never does the obvious things that might resolve the problem of choice. She does nothing about the letter from the school; she does not show it to Mrs. Grose, and we are ourselves prevented from judging the nature of its contents. She does not write to the boy's uncle about it; she does not write to the school authorities to inquire of them the exact cause for his dismissal; she does not question Miles himself. Yet the perfect trust on which this attitude seems to be based is ready to yield to its opposite. The gentleness of the children is called 'a trap that put her off her guard', the peacefulness of the succeeding days, 'the hush in which something gathers or crouches'.

When she has her first vision of the man on the tower, she does not make general inquiry about a possible intruder, but only after the figure's second appearance speaks to Mrs. Grose about the being she describes as 'a horror', or 'like nobody', as though he could not be identified in ordinary human terms.

Miles, meanwhile, continues to astound her by his perfect goodness, which she scrutinizes for evidences of its opposite:

> If he had been wicked he would have 'caught' it, and I should have caught it by the rebound—I should have found the trace, should have felt the wound and the dishonour. I could reconstitute nothing at all, and he was therefore an angel.

Without warrant, it would seem, then, she 'knows' that there has been something between Miles and the dead valet, and that the spectre is trying to continue relations—and her suspicion is confirmed by Mrs. Grose's revelation, to her 'sickness of disgust', that, alive, Quint had been 'too free'. So Miles is corrupt after all! She begins to watch the children with an attentiveness of suspicion that she calls a 'service admirable and difficult', a devoted guardianship, but her own words betray her: 'I began to watch them in a stifled suspense, a disguised tension, that might well, had it continued too long, have turned into something like madness.' And what 'saved' her from this madness, the madness of being unable to move from the pole of trust to the pole of condemnation? Why, 'proofs' of the children's infernal natures, the first of these being the appearance of Miss Jessel and Flora's appearance of pretending that she has not seen this female figure of 'quite as unmistakable horror and evil'. But she will not confirm or dismiss her hypothesis by questioning the child herself.

The alternatives are, as always, absolutes. If the child meets the dead governess willingly, is it not, asks Mrs. Grose, 'just proof of her blest innocence?' But the governess counters: 'If it isn't a proof of what you say, it's a proof of—God knows what! For the woman is a horror of horrors.' At this point, the governess announces, 'It's far worse than I dreamed. They're lost.' So the governess has moved from her vision of perfect goodness to its opposite. But now it is her own worth and validity that she describes in the self-contradictory language that suggests negation even as it affirms, as in the following which pretends to exonerate Flora:

> To gaze into the depths of the child's eyes and to pronounce their loveliness a trick of premature cunning was to be guilty of a cynicism in preference to which I naturally preferred to abjure my judgment.

In the presence of the children, however, the see-saw is again in motion, and 'everything fell to the ground but their incapacity and their beauty', until, as it swings back to the negative side she feels 'obliged to re-investigate the certitude' of Flora's 'inconceivable communion'.

By questioning Mrs. Grose she ascertains, to her satisfaction, that Miles had known about the relation between Quint and Miss Jessel and had concealed this knowledge and been corrupted by it. It is no use for Mrs. Grose to cry, 'If he was so bad then as that comes to, how is he such an angel now?' Everything the governess now thinks she learns about the relations of the children and the dead pair suits 'exactly the particular deadly view [she is] in the very act of forbidding [herself] to entertain'. She resolves to wait for the evidence of Miles's damnation. Even as she waits, however, the effect of her pupils' appearance gives a 'brush of the sponge' to her convictions and she begins 'to struggle against [her] new lights'. Their charm, as it maintains itself, seems 'a beguilement still effective even under the shadow of a possibility that it was studied'. Their graceful responsiveness to her succeeds 'as if [she] never appeared . . . literally to catch them at a purpose in it'. 'If' the children 'practised upon [her], it was surely with the minimum of grossness'.

It is then she has her third encounter with Quint and finds that Flora, at the window, denies that she has seen or looked for anyone but the governess herself—who reflects, 'I absolutely believed she lied.' And she sees Miss Jessel on the stairs before, on another night, the little girl is again at the window, and the governess declares with conviction, 'She was face to face with the apparition we had met at the lake and could now communicate with it as she had not then been able to do.' She herself sees only little Miles in the garden, but is convinced that he is gazing up at the tower above her head, the tower at the top of which, standing in the same spot, she had herself seen the valet's ghost. So the governess concludes and concludes, and her images betray her self-knowledge or her suspicion of absolute evil in herself when she describes how Mrs. Grose listened to her 'disclosures', her theories. It was, she says, 'as had I wished to mix a witch's broth and propose it with assurance, she would have held out a large clean saucepan.'

Miles's explanation is the very centre of the story, the nub of the problem I have been describing as the governess's absolutist obsession. He tells her that he simply wanted to bring down a little her conception of his unnatural goodness, to make her think him 'for a change—*bad!*' He had been very naughty; he had sat up without undressing until midnight, and then he had gone out and nearly caught cold. 'When I'm bad I *am* bad!' he says, in triumph. And she is nearly persuaded to see-saw once again thinking of 'all the reserves of goodness that, for his joke, he had been able to draw upon'. But she returns to her conviction that the children are engaged in a continuous deception and that 'the four . . . perpetually meet.' She tells Mrs. Grose: 'Their more than earthly beauty, their absolutely unnatural goodness. It's a game. It's a policy and a fraud!' Miles's plea for a normal human allowance of good and bad comingled has failed.

Yet more and more her language betrays that she, who has dreamed the rôle of saviour, has become by her own converting vision, demonic. 'It was not, I am sure today, then, my mere infernal imagination', she declares, or, after she sees Miss Jessel at her desk, 'she was there, so I was justified, she was there, so I was neither cruel nor mad.' Against the weak denial of the syntax the powerful epithets, 'infernal', 'cruel', 'mad' thrust themselves. The children continue affectionate, and she says, 'Adorable they must in truth have been, I now feel, since I didn't in those days hate them!'—and we are made to suspect that hate them she did and does. Miles's reasonable plea for school and his liberty arouses her determination to prevent it, it would seem, for *now* she will write the master and inform him of the expulsion from the old school. Again, when Mrs. Grose asks the nature of the child's offense, she—and we—are denied, and the governess answers in terms, once more, of the evil-goodness alternatives: 'For wickedness. For what else—when he's so clever and beautiful and perfect?' Only abstract wickedness can be the counter-truth of such an appearance of completest goodness. She is driven now, beyond her former discretion, to even ask him what had happened and to receive for answer only his shriek as she appeals to him, drops on her knees, to 'seize once more the chance of possessing him', and he blows out the candle—or Quint does. The admission, the proof absolute, still evades her while she reflects,

> Say that, by the dark prodigy I knew the imagination of all evil *had* been opened to him; all the justice within me ached for the proof that it could ever have flowered into act.

And so the children continue *either* divine or infernal, as the governess's use of the words betrays. She calls their contrivance to keep her from simultaneously observing them (Miles plays the piano for her while Flora goes off to the lake), 'the most divine little way to keep me quiet'. 'Divine?' echoes Mrs. Grose, and the governess rather giddily responds, 'Infernal then!' The governess is now ready to speak out, to say, 'Miss Jessel', to Flora, and point to the opposite bank of the lake with triumph and even 'gratitude' that the apparition is there and the moment of proof has arrived, but the child sees nothing and says to Mrs. Grose, who sees nothing also, 'Take me away from *her!*'

There is nothing more to be hoped for from Flora, and she must be taken away by Mrs. Grose, who gives the governess what 'justifies' her when she reports the 'horrors'—again undenotable—that she has heard from the child. She is, consequently, alone with Miles, still to extract a confession from him. She is assailed by a 'perverse horror' of her own efforts:

> for what did it consist of but the obtrusion of the idea of grossness and guilt on a small helpless creature who had been for me a revelation of the possibilities of beautiful intercourse?

But the illumination passes. She asks him if he stole her letter and Quint's 'white face of damnation' appears at the window once more just as the boy admits that he has taken it. And then she asks him what he had done at school and gets only his vague reply that he 'said things . . . to those I liked'. It sounds altogether so meagre a criminality that the governess swings, for the last time, away from her conviction of his depravity and feels 'the appalling alarm of his being perhaps innocent. It was for an instant confounding and bottomless, for if he were innocent what then on earth was I?' It is *her* innocence, finally, that may be its opposite, that is, damnation. And this, in fact, is what she must find confirmed at the very last. Pointing to the wraith she sees at the window, clasping the terrified child to her breast, she hears him cry out, 'Peter Quint—you devil!' She has triumphed; it is 'a tribute to her devotion'; she has named the 'hideous author of our woe', almost identified, in the Miltonic phrase, with the Devil himself. *Or* she has been herself named the devil of the story, she who has believed in the absolute beauty of childish innocence, in the master's unimpugnable grace, in her own holy motives—for Miles, who sees nothing that she sees, is dead.

# 4

# 'Nothing that is not there and the nothing that is': The Celebration of Absence in *The Wings of the Dove*

## by NICOLA BRADBURY

T. S. Eliot, whose work reverberates with echoes of Henry James, epitomized the notion that 'In my end is my beginning'. In two of James's novels the last sentences are so close that one sounds like a re-working of the other; or, to put it another way, the earlier is implicit in the later, and we are left with the question whether this novel did not begin with the sense of its ending. Direction, implicit in the sequence of a text, suggests purpose. In criticism we avoid dullness of Popeian proportions when the end is where we start from. Is it so in James's fiction, whose self-critical qualities are notorious? This suggestion of teleology runs counter to the allure of free play amongst ideas and the formulation of ideas, a concept I take to be central to Derrida's *différance*, which embraces both distinction and deferral of meaning.[1] That *différance*, and its concomitant *absence* of logocentrism governed by subjective intention, would seem useful concepts in reading late James; but can they be reconciled, or must they be modified, or supersede, the quality James thought implicit in any work of art: the quality of mind of the producer?[2] *The Wings of the Dove* ends with Kate Croy's elegiac recognition, 'We shall never be again as we were!' and this echoes, but changes, Strether's conclusion to *The Ambassadors* (published later but written earlier): 'Then there we are!' In *The Wings of the Dove*, that fixity of time and place in an eternal present has altered to the ellipsis of future ('we shall . . . be') and past ('as we were') which articulates through the tenses of the verb the recognition also voiced in the negative ('never') of a felt absence: the absence of Milly, and of the possibilities of life she represents.

What I should like to do in this paper is examine the kind of satisfaction James offers through this conclusion (surely deliberate, as the echo suggests), and to see how James's technique, shifting from *The Ambassdors* into *The Wings of the Dove* (and on into *The Golden Bowl*, which I do not propose to tackle here), explores the possibilities of balancing closure (the sense of an ending) against *différance* (endless change) in the celebration of absence as a positive joy through the text. The end of *The Wings of the Dove* brings an excitement not available in Strether's acceptance of where he stands; and for Maggie Verver, the knowledge of limitation gives a liberating power. The working of the text offers a metaphor of fitness—not perhaps the dictation of what is right, but the articulation of what is possible—for in each novel the interplay of protagonist and experience mediates that of author, reader and text, in a sophisticated, and delightful, intertextuality which exploits the power and the vulnerability of each position. This, for James, is the 'interest' of the 'process and the effect of representation'.[3]

In critical terms this could be charted as the movement from structuralism in *The Ambassadors* towards deconstruction in *The Golden Bowl*. Todorov[4] has offered structuralist readings of some middle James works and short stories affirming their diacritical quality: texts intricate with self-referentiality and alert to the fragility of an external 'real thing'. This system works brilliantly in the areas Todorov explores, and it maps in James's fiction the literary finesse of the innovator. It could be extended perhaps to *The Ambassadors*, where Strether painstakingly learns exactly to read his own experience, only to find this entails writing himself out of any alternative. But by the time of *The Golden Bowl*, James's protagonist Maggie Verver has mastered deconstruction (the reading the text demands—including its multiple conflicting possibilities) only to reassert a prior formulation (the authorial text); and her authority for this lies precisely in her own self-consciousness: the awareness of the limitations imposed by the individual self. The challenge is to place *The Wings of the Dove* in the context of this shifting fictional process, to see how far the novel depends upon liberation, even through disaster, from the structuralist system, and the apprehension, through mortality, of a sense of time and change, a sense of process which is marked through the subject (victim and agent) of experience: the irreplaceable self, most valued in its absence, since here the fullness of presence is most purely implied.

James's monograph on *Hawthorne* (1879) gives early evidence of his interest in the concept of absence. He clearly valued it with pre-structuralist prescience:

> [Hawthorne] was silent, diffident, more inclined to hesitate, to watch and wait and meditate, than to produce himself, and fonder, on almost any occasion, of being absent than of being present. This quality betrays itself in all his writings.[5]

Absence, which is vital to *The Wings of the Dove* as a value both in structure and tone, is already a factor in *The Ambassadors*, and perhaps a determining force. Strether's wife and son, Marie de Vionnet's husband (and Mrs. Newsome's, and Maria Gostrey's) are absences from the cast list. Mrs. Newsome's absence is a calculated pressure on Strether, and on the text. The absence of statement from the lovers is the key to the plot. But there are also different, less agressive aspects of absence: Strether's Hawthorne-like hesitancy, which gives space to the text; and within that space, the half-sensed lack, for Strether, finally fully recognized, of triumphant Life, with all that it involves.

E. M. Forster's 'hourglass' image of the plot will also do to figure this aspect of the novel, which inverts the concept of absence, from a felt lack, to the grateful condition, for Strether, of freedom, and hence of being. This is what we need to recognize in order to read Strether's last scenes as anything other than disaster: the positive aspect of his final affirmation, 'That, you see, is my only logic. Not, out of the whole affair, to have got anything for myself.' This conclusion is secure if we share Strether's point of view, and James uses a series of devices to ensure that as the novel develops we will. A 'system of differences' ranging from plot and scene to individual words and images articulates possibility in *The Ambassadors*, and directs the movement from misunderstanding to comprehension. The transition from innocence to knowledge is an experience anticipated, then shared, by reader and protagonist. The final aim is the freedom from limitations, but the means involve recognition of the impossible, the false position, and that is why the quality of absence dominant in the text, and still threatening perhaps at the end, can be characterized by the first part of Wallace Stevens's line as 'Nothing that is not there': it is truth by negative definition.

Knowledge in *The Ambassadors* delineates falsehood, prevarication and inadequacy, but moves towards the negative apprehension (in their absence) of positive values; and this is a movement which grows more vigorous, dangerous and exhilarating in *The Wings of the Dove*, for which I have appropriated the second part of Wallace Stevens's line, with its absolute and joyful paradox, 'the nothing that is'.

We can trace progress relatively easily through *The Ambassadors*, where meaning systems interlock through their shared characteristic of duality, the ambiguity that enables Strether, and the reader, to go from one reading of experience to another. This direction requires things to be 'placed' in their proper relation, both to each other and to the observer. James's most economical imagery for this process is pictorial: from named works of art or picturesque narrative moments to the rules of composition, colouring, light, perspective, and framing. The 'picture of the stage' with Maria Gostrey in London gives way to Strether's 'Lambinet' in the French countryside, and one kind of pretence supersedes another. After that day, Strether is figured as a connoisseur:

> Between nine and ten, at last, in the high clear picture—he was moving in these days, as in a gallery, from clever canvas to clever canvas—he drew a long breath: it was so presented to

85

him from the first that the spell of his luxury wouldn't be broken.

In their last interview, Marie de Vionnet is 'framed' by her surroundings, as Maria Gostrey is to be by hers, though the style, French Romantic and Dutch interior, is distinctly different. On this occasion Strether is beset by intimations of absence: 'He should soon be going to where such things were not.' Then, in Maria's rooms, he has a fuller critical understanding of the offered structure—but he also conceives a reason for rejection:

> It built him softly round, it roofed him warmly over, it rested, all so firm, on selection. And what ruled selection was beauty and knowledge. It was awkward, it was almost stupid, not to seem to prize such things; yet, none the less, so far as they made his opportunity they made it only for a moment.

Selection constructs beauty and knowledge, but its scope is of the moment. The future offers a larger absence, 'where such things were not'. In that context, we can return to the concluding sentence of the novel, which I have described as a closure of space and time in the recognition of the present, and notice more accurately how some hope is opened even here. Finality may be left behind with the text; this is the possibility sustained by the insignificant introductory word, which hints at a statute of limitations and violates with colloquial ease the tense of the verb: '*Then* there we are!'

Time, which is doom in *The Wings of the Dove*, is not absent from *The Ambassadors*. For Strether in conversation at Gloriani's garden party, youth was the moment of lost opportunity, and he presses little Bilham to take advantage of it:

> Still, one has the illusion of freedom; therefore don't be, like me, without the memory of that illusion. I was either, at the right time, too stupid or too intelligent to have it; I don't quite know which. Of course at present I'm a case of reaction against the mistake. . . .

Though the text is contained in time, and moments are marked and named, days, hours, there is a sense of suspended duration in Strether's prolonged innocence, and only with knowledge does he witness the desperation of Marie and crass casualty of Chad faced with old age. The book enjoys a comic immunity to temporal decay; yet its plot unfolds in sequence, and Strether learns gradually, that this experience in the privileged Old World must be integrated with the New, and with the rest of his doings and his being there.

There can be no question that *The Wings of the Dove* is a tragedy; yet *différance* permits not only the challenge of domestic and grotesque comedy but the pantomime postures of romance a forceful presence in the work. This deliberate adoption of conflicting and minor modes, whose artificialities spangle the text, signals a deconstructive, rather than structuralist, proceeding. Instead of the central consciousness (Strether) learning the system of signification to master experience, we have a protagonist (Milly) who does not enter the novel until the third book (of ten), and leaves well before the last. She is, moreover, isolated, by nationality, wealth, sex, illness. She is surrounded by those who have a use for her, whether benevolent or exploitative, and who would like to put her into their own structures of significance, governed by subjective intention. It is Milly's distinction that she recognizes not only this but, more remarkably, the extent to which the same could be said to be true for those manipulating her. Her doom gives her the detachment from the system in which 'the working and the worked were . . . the parties to every relation', just as her fate detaches her bodily from the text in progress. Instead of a meaningful system (perhaps the romantic courtship rewarded in marriage) Milly recognizes the conflict of intentions, relations and possibilities, and the arbitrary nature of the ending (not her desire, but extinction). Paradoxically, the condition of her perception, her consciousness, is also the condition of its insecurity. How is Milly to be vindicated, her consciousness validated, if what it indicates to her is true, and she is to die alone?

The triumph of *The Wings of the Dove* is to achieve precisely this through the paradox of absence, in which Milly (and all she stands for) is more powerful, pure and true, than in mere presence; she has moved out of time and transcends the working world. The habits of reading engendered in the extravagance of the texture of *différance* enable us to encompass this supreme paradox. But Milly's survivors are left without the means to validate their interpretation of experience: a difficulty brilliantly dramatized in the scene where Kate takes from Densher (it is Christmas, the season of gifts) Milly's sealed announcement of her will, and 'jerked the thing into the flame'. It is not through any action or intention of Milly's, but through their own apprehension of it, that the others must come to a valuation of her, in her absence. Only this can exhaust presuppositions to allow them a sense of themselves; and it is this sense, movingly caught in the gap between future and past, that Kate voices in her conclusion that 'We shall never be again as we were!'

Only complete readings can properly try the suggestion that structuralism in *The Ambassadors* gives way to deconstruction in *The Wings of the Dove*; but it is possible even in limited space both to contrast the use of comparable image-clusters in the novels, and to go on to explore the expansion, or the explosion, of technique. We need not belittle *The Ambassadors* (which James himself considered 'frankly, quite the best, "all round", of my productions') in order to enjoy *The Wings of the Dove* to the full; but it is exciting to move, as James did, on from one achievement to the next, and to find how it is that this moves us.

The first shock in *The Wings of the Dove* comes with the domestic sordidness of the opening book, and an encounter between Kate Croy and her father which recalls that between Maisie and Beale Farange, but stripped of its tawdry exoticism. Kate's response to this murkiness is structuralist abstraction and determination. She sees history as a text, musical or verbal, seeks motive, and the prize of meaning. So she is dissatisfied with the sense that

> the whole history of their house had the effect of some fine florid, voluminous phrase, say even a musical, that dropped first into words, into notes, without sense, and then, hanging unfinished, into no words, no notes at all.

She asks,

> Why should a set of people have been put in motion, on such a scale and with such an air of being equipped for a profitable journey, only to break down without an accident, to stretch themselves in the wayside dust without a reason?

And she decides, 'She hadn't given up yet, and the broken sentence, if she was the last word, *would* end with a sort of meaning.' All this sounds like self-referentiality in the text, prompting recognition of Kate's authority, through an inwardness between her, the author and the reader, in the conjoint activities of invention and interpretation in the construction of meaning. So Kate is to be our 'fine consciousness'? What—apart from the obvious signals in the surroundings—is there to hint that this may not be so: that this may be an inappropriate procedure here?

Not, at this stage, very much. The signs of Kate's intelligence are subtle, varied and persuasive—though it is true that intelligence is a quality even Lionel Croy cannot be said to lack. But we are given clues that Kate's reading may not be authoritative, and even, more importantly, that no single reading may be definitive, in the way that Strether's final understanding in *The Ambassadors* approaches completeness. Ian Watt's seminal paper on 'The First Paragraph of *The Ambassadors*: An Explication' (*Essays in Criticism*, X (1960), 250–74) pointed out how James includes directions for reading as well as a foretaste of the action in the opening sentence, which begins, 'Strether's first question'. The novel asks questions and looks for answers. Kate, too, asks questions, as we have seen; but the novel declines to accord them the same status as Strether's. Her questions (the questions she might have in mind) hang in the air, not only unanswered, but unasked. They crop up, the first of a series in the text, not as part of a process of investigation, but as instruments of discomfiture. Questions abound, but the thing is not to suppose that solves anything.

> The answer to these questions was not in Chirk Street, but the questions themselves bristled there, and the girl's repeated pause before the mirror and the chimney-place might have represented her nearest approach to an escape from them.

Kate's escape is to offer her own answer, the sentence which '*would* end with a sort of meaning'. But the deconstructive text does not work in this way; rather, it follows William James's 'pragmatic method'. Kate cherishes 'the name, above all, she would take in hand—the precious name she so liked and that, in spite of the harm her wretched father had done it, was not yet past praying for'. William James, in *Pragmatism: A New Name for Some Old Ways of Thinking* (1909), was to write:

> Solomon knew the names of all the spirits, so having their names, he held them subject to his will. So the universe has always appeared to the natural mind as a kind of enigma, of which the key must be sought in the shape of some illuminating of power-bringing word or name. . . . But if you follow the pragmatic method, you cannot look on any such word as closing your quest. You must bring out of each word its practical cash-value, set it at work within the stream of your experience. It appears less as a solution, then, than as a programme for more work, and particularly as an indication of the ways in which existing realities may be *changed*.

Language, and linguistic terms, is one of the ways in which *The Wings of the Dove* both invites and frustrates a structuralist, logo-centric reading. After the introduction of Kate in the first book comes Densher to share the second book, and sustain the supposition (only later to be overturned) that these will be the conventional 'hero' and 'heroine' of our tale. Densher, like Kate, is a sophisticated reader of signs. But his confrontation with Aunt Maud, like Kate's with Lionel Croy, shows comically how two can play at that game, and expertise in interpreting experience brings no power in a world of conflicting languages: 'He read more vividly, more critically, as has been hinted, the appearances about him; and they did nothing so much as make him wonder at his aesthetic reaction.' The linguistic, indeed structuralist, terms, are inescapable:

> It was the language of the house itself that spoke to him, writing out for him, with surpassing breadth and freedom, the associations and conceptions, the ideals and possibilities of the mistress. . . . These things finally represented for him a por- tentous negation of his own world of thought—of which, for that matter, in the presence of them, he became as for the first time hopelessly aware. They revealed it to him by their merciless difference.

The use of language against itself, to reveal and negate presuppositions, is the cleverest of a series of techniques for deconstruction. On a larger scale the possibilities of different narrative modes are played off against each other, to similarly explosive effect. The 'realism' of Chirk Street and of 'comfortless Chelsea' with their 'glazed cloth' and 'the lingering odour of boiled food' is an opportunity to flirt with vulgarity exposed; but the materials of Balzac, if not Zola, are converted by a narrative spell into the stuff of Cinderella's kitchen; and when Susan Stringham and Milly Theale arrive in Europe, trailing literary associations from the Tauchnitz to echoes of the Bible, but cherishing an appetite for the romantic abyss and fairy-tale figures, they join a scene already well prepared. It is not a fairy-tale world, but one capable of that disguise as of many others. Though the romance mode is one James particularly exploits, it is not this but the matter of exploitation itself that characterizes the text. Language, narrative mode, imagery, all contribute to this exuberance, and it is often very funny: the foreground of pathos, once Milly enters. Two sentences will convey the vigour of the opening books. Each is devoted to a decidedly minor character, promoted, for this moment of the narrative, to overwhelming stature. It is the range of imagery, the artful control, through rhythm, syntax and alliteration, of the phonic qualities of language and the witty interplay of ideas, which together justify Lionel Croy through his own vitality:

> This was the weariness of every fresh meeting; he dealt out lies as he might the cards from the greasy old pack for the game of diplomacy to which you were to sit down with him.

As for Aunt Maud: James creates a sense of her enormity, not only through simile, but through the internal extravagances, the inconsistencies, of his description. On the one hand it is an affair of abstracts:

> It was by her personality that Aunt Maud was prodigious, and the great mass of it loomed because, in the thick, the foglike air of her arranged existence, there were parts doubtless magnified and parts certainly vague.

On the other hand, Aunt Maud has such surfaces that no depths can possibly be imagined behind them:

> She would have been meanwhile a wonderful lioness for a show, an extraordinary figure in a cage or anywhere; majestic,

91

magnificent, high-coloured, all brilliant gloss, perpetual satin, twinkling bugles and flashing gems, with a lustre of agate eyes, a sheen of raven hair, a polish of complexion that was like that of well-kept china and that—as if the skin were too tight—told especially at curves and corners.

Undaunted by such monstrosities, when Milly emerges from the protection of Susan Stringham into the London world in Book Fourth, her narrative début is at a dinner party where 'Milly made out these things—with a shade of exhilaration at the way she already fell in—she saw how she was justified of her plea for people and her love of life.' The language of experience is reminiscent of Strether's initiation: 'The smallest things . . . were all touches in a picture and denotements in a play; and they marked for her, moreover, her alertness of vision.' Urgency, for Milly, is the condition of being, but the pressure is still towards interpretation:

> Nothing was so odd as that she should have to recognize so quickly in each of these glimpses of an instant the various signs of a relation; and this anomaly itself, had she had more time to give to it, might well, might almost terribly have suggested to her that her doom was to live fast. It was queerly a question of the short run and the consciousness proportionately crowded.

The 'question' here is quite devoid of any interrogative element; it is nearer an imperative. Under these circumstances, Milly's achievement is not to master the techniques of interpretation, despite her obvious flair for this game of 'relation'. It is to see where the game ends. Though she could do it, it would do her no good. Two things above all convey this perception: very different kinds of insight, one very public, the other utterly private: the vision of the Bronzino, and the vision of Kate.

A jealous apprehension is what alerts Milly to the 'otherness' in Kate, but the perception is distinguished precisely by a capacity to see round selfishness: not to transcend or negate it, but to fix it, give it due acknowledgement, understand:

> She should never know how Kate truly felt about anything such a one as Milly Theale should give her to feel. Kate would never—and not from ill-will, nor from duplicity, but from a sort of failure of common terms—reduce it to such a one's comprehension or put it within her convenience.

The use of her own full name and of the impersonality of the generalizing 'such a one' here is wonderfully tactful. Milly's perception is lifted from the occasional to a law of consciousness: that it is limited, and exclusive. Hence her sense of Kate on occasion as 'appearing at a given moment to show as a beautiful stranger . . . who was above all a subject for curiosity'. Since Kate's otherness is inviolable, Milly can without impropriety—and without hope—speculate on her relationship with Densher: ' "Is it the way she looks to *him?*" she asked herself—the perversity being that she kept in remembrance that Kate was known to him.' Milly's self-punishment (she lays herself open to harm by asking Kate for help in seeing her doctor) is not a price, but a tribute, to this higher consciousness: the consciousness of personal absence, the condition of individual being.

The Bronzino scene performs a similar act of deconstruction in relation to a work of art. The fifth book, which begins with the day at Matcham and ends in the National Gallery encounter of Milly with Kate and Densher, and embraces the interview with Sir Luke Strett and Milly's subsequent walk through 'the grey immensity of London', coming to terms with the fact of death amidst 'the practical question of life'; the book as a whole, rich in beauty and pathos, could be seen as the setting of one moment: the moment when Milly faces the Bronzino portrait. Her readiness for this critical encounter can be inferred from the sophistication (long unattainable by Strether) with which she understands, as a post-structuralist might, 'that this largeness of style was the sign of *appointed* felicity'. Having italicized the signal word, James immediately repeats his phrase, to make the point again: 'The largeness of style was the great containing vessel.' Though Milly is by no means insensitive to that style, though she is carried along, as the text is, in the luxury of the occasion, the moment of 'apotheosis', however liberated from subjective intention, is 'good', 'beautiful', 'right', precisely because it exactly detaches itself from what is 'appointed'. James's description of the portrait is carefully controlled, and almost spare, in deference to the quality of the work; yet nevertheless there is such an intensity of apprehension in this description that the subject and object of vision (Milly and the Bronzino) are fused, and it is impossible securely to say which is 'the lady in question' during the encounter. Milly herself, however, is not confused. The distinction between them is that the Bronzino 'was a very great personage—only unaccompanied by a joy', but Milly has the joy of deconstruction: 'Milly recognized her exactly in words that had nothing to do with her.'

This remarkable sentence, not susceptible to conventional interpretation, liberates recognition from definition (limitation, or ending). It is the conjunction between this arbitrary play with significance and Milly's statement itself that has provoked endless critical speculation over the 'meaning' of this scene. Milly's words seem to affirm a logical pattern of comparison which contradicts the flagrant disparity of comment earlier asserted. 'I shall never be better than this', she says, and critics, like Lord Mark, have wondered what 'better' compares with, and what 'this' refers to. But such questions have their rebuttal in the text (nicely contained in the dismissive pluperfect): 'He hadn't understood.' The point is the absence of straightforward reference 'in words that had nothing to do with her'. To have 'nothing to do with' frees subject and object from the restrictions of 'relation', and from the dangers of manipulation—for 'the working and the worked were . . . the parties to every relation', as the London season has taught Milly. The Bronzino scene, which might have been a definitive exercise, finding the perfect image for the heroine, and thus framing her in the narrative, is turned instead into the active negation of such procedures, through the assertion of difference and the celebration of absence.

The apotheosis at Matcham has been read as a paradigm of which another variant is the 'Veronese' dinner party in Venice; and this might seem to contradict any possibility of freeplay. But the scenes are very different. They share the attribute of likeness to a painting, announced by an attendant character, 'framing' Milly. In the first, she escapes through her own act of deconstruction. Later, the narrative itself preserves her space: Milly is the object of veneration, celebration, speculation; but she is passive, worked round. Her party is the occasion for Kate and Densher to come to their arrangement:

'On your honour?'
'On my honour.'
'You'll come?'
'I'll come.'

When Kate has come and gone, the next book opens with a brilliant ellipsis, and a signalling pluperfect. The words which follow those just quoted (after the chapter/book break) are: 'It was after they had gone that he truly felt the difference.' This is the beginning of Densher's slow apprehension of what 'difference' marks, as he enters his false position, and feels the world of forms is his structure of betrayal. Having had Kate, he finds the emptiness of presence:

> He had, in fine, judged his friend's pledge in advance as an inestimable value, and what he must not know his case for was that of a possession of the value to the full. Wasn't it perhaps even rather the value that possessed *him*, kept him thinking of it and waiting on it, turning round and round it and making sure of it again from this side and that?

The rest of the novel twists and turns in this way as Densher and Kate make their bid for Milly, and Densher comes to recognize the impossibility of his position. His first sign of grace is in staying away from the Palazzo; turning away is Milly's last sign; when Densher returns to London, Kate greets him, 'Then it has been—what do you say? a whole fortnight?—without your making a sign?' Their 'wonderful system' is intact for her, but for Densher it is already ruined. As the narrative closes in, both in terms of plot and, correspondingly, space, and actors, Densher's imagination stretches:

> It was in seeing her that he felt what their interruption had been, and that they met across it even as persons whose adventures, on either side, in time and space, of the nature of perils and exiles, had had a peculiar strangeness. He wondered if he were as different for her as she herself had immediately appeared. . . .

Though the text abounds in terms which have an uncannily post-modern tone—difference, absence, strangeness, sign, system—it would be deeply misleading to suggest that these amount to the attribution of a capacity for deconstruction in either Kate or Densher. They are both, though to different degrees, lost, in a mapless London park, like the one Milly wandered through, confronted by silence, non-communication, moral and emotional uncertainty. Kate can cry out in defiance of conventional morality and conventional meaning systems, 'She never wanted the truth . . . She wanted *you*.' This is the assertion of romantic love, nullifying morality. Densher, however, has a deeper unease, and this is nearer the necessary chaos of the text. The tenth book moves slowly, but dreadfully, towards the alienation of Kate and Densher, and their recognition of it, which is a horror not all their new politeness can contain. Here words fail:

> It had come to the point, really, that they showed each other pale faces, and that all the unspoken between them looked out of their eyes in a dim terror of their further conflict.

These depths escape superficial dangers, however: 'It was blessed at least that all ironies failed them, and during another slow moment their very sense of it cleared the air.' Nevertheless, they do not understand each other, and their final echo,

> 'As we were?'
> 'As we were.'

is capped by a delicately staged exit: 'But she turned to the door, and her headshake was now the end. "We shall never be again as we were!"'

The positive effects of this conclusion are not susceptible of quotation in the way that these textual circumstances are, for the absence of Milly is one enacted by the text. It is not a case of simple binary opposition: Kate/Milly, live/dead, present/absent. The effect of all those terms of absence in the text, not part of the characterization of the lovers, is to underline the inefficacy of all systems. Milly is triumphant, not because she has bested Kate in death, but because she has escaped all systems. The wistfulness of Kate's last words is her tribute to what she cannot apprehend; but they cannot be called definitive. Their effect, wonderfully, is to throw the reader back into the text, in the same movement as ushering both reader and character out.

# The Celebration of Absence in 'The Wings of the Dove'

## NOTES

1. There is a brief, accessible introduction to Derrida's notion of *différance* in 'Structuralism and post-structuralism' by Ann Jefferson, *Modern Literary Theory: A Comparative Introduction*, ed. Ann Jefferson and David Robey (London: Batsford Academic and Educational Ltd., 1982), pp. 104–6. Disciples of Derrida deny the validity of his terms taken out of context and used as linguistic counters in the logo-centric systems of traditional criticism. In this paper, however, my aim is to refer through these terms to the open possibilities of deconstruction, and not to restrict their significance.
2. 'The Art of Fiction', *Henry James: Selected Literary Criticism*, ed. Morris Shapira (1963; rpt. 1968), p. 96.
3. Henry James, Preface to *The Golden Bowl* (New York, 1909).
4. Tzvetan Todorov, 'The Structural Analysis of Literature: Henry James', *Structuralism: An Introduction* (Oxford, 1973), pp. 73–101.
5. Henry James, *Hawthorne* (1879); with an introduction and notes by Tony Tanner (London: Macmillan, 1967), p. 42.

# 5

# 'The Intimate Difference': Power and Representation in *The Ambassadors*

by MAUD ELLMANN

Once upon a time, two artists challenged one another to create the most impenetrable illusion. The grapes that Zeuxis painted looked so lusciously alive that the birds swooped down to pluck them off the vine. But his rival, Parrhasios, knew that verisimilitude is for the birds. Rather than imitate appearances he painted a veil upon a wall that looked as thought it swathed the truth in gossamer. The prurient Zeuxis demanded that the veil be drawn aside so that he could see whatever it was hiding.

It is precisely because Zeuxis refuses to be duped that Parrhasios can ensnare him in his veil. In the paranoia of interpretation he transforms the picture into a sign, which veils its inner meaning in its outer cerements. Lacan argues that 'the picture does not compete with appearances', for it competes with the Idea that Plato wrapped behind the world.[1] But this old story also hints that Plato would have never dreamed of the Idea had he not painted veils for it to hide behind.

*1*

This fable could have prefaced *The Ambassadors* if James had not already crammed his book with prolegomena. He even called the text itself a 'supplement'.[2] His Project prognosticates the text, but also turns into its rival; for as it stretched to its prodigious length, it also grew more novelistic than the novel. There is more story in the Project than the finished work, more fiction in the introductions and the postscripts. What the Project fills in, the novel hollows out, as if it were editing its own critique. The fiction shrinks behind the veil of its own representations of itself.

Veiled without, the text is also lined with veils within, for representation is its central theme as well as its cocoon. *The Ambassadors* explores two forms of representation—aesthetic and political—together with the ways in which they implicate each other. In politics, ambassadors forsake their place of origin to represent their countrymen abroad. Similarly, a work of art is thought to represent the mind that made it or the world that made the mind. And yet the image, too, relinquishes its own original, for that which must live immortal in art must perish in life. In both cases, the symbol supplements the power that it represents, and extends its influence beyond the presence of its source. But it also mocks the dream that any power is sufficient to itself. The very words for representatives, like 'members' or 'detachments', whisper that they mutilate their origins. The power they disseminate is ruptured from the moment that it represents itself. As soon as there is representation there is treason, for nothing can be doubled unless it has already double-crossed itself.

Mrs. Newsome is a falling monarch. The kind of power that she represents is wracked with neurasthenia. Under monarchy it is assumed that the representative reflects his sovereign's image faithfully, in the same way that an artist pledges his fidelity to life. But Mrs. Newsome's representatives apostasize their cause and mock mimesis. Their waywardness suggests that monarchism can no longer delimit the effects of a decentralized and circulating power. In the place of the unique form of a great power a field of forces has arisen where power fluctuates and swirls. Mobile, multiplicitous, these forces shift about, disbanding and regrouping in a dance of difference. Instead of descending from above, power surges from below, fretful with its own negativity.[3] While the sovereign exercises power as repression, Strether represents the power of surveillance; and rather than repressing Chad's delights, he opens up new byways of desire.

Two representations sally forth to Paris, for it is part of the 'strange logic' (60) of the text that every incident repeats or represents itself.[4] First, Strether is dispatched with Waymarsh to rescue Chad, so as to save his mother's moral and financial empire. Because he is bewitched by the savages he was commissioned to revile, the Pococks put to sea to save the missionaries. These two delegations cross swords in the name of two hostile powers, which bring to pass opposing forms of knowledge and pleasure. The Pococks relish closure. But Strether falls in love with ambiguity, till every thing he sees becomes the sign that veils some rich, dark mystery. The world twinkles with alterity. What Chad is, or what he was, enraptures Strether less than his facility to differ from himself. The other emissaries can only read Chad's difference as perfidy. He has flouted the values he should represent, and the economy of representation demands his realignment with his mother as urgently as the economy of Woollett does. To save Chad would save mimesis, which Mrs. Newsome's throne depends upon. If the vagabonds returned to their origins, the signifier would be reconciled to the signified.

For the fate of meaning is at stake. James called his novel a 'drama of discrimination' (7), and Strether must discriminate between two forms of meaning, only one of which can countenance desire. His mission leads him into an adventure of interpretation, for he transforms the streets of Paris into the defiles of the signifier. Chad himself becomes a book, revised by the subtlest of editors. ' "I'm not sure he was meant by nature to be quite so good," ' says little Bilham. ' "It's like the new edition of an old book that one has been fond of—revised and amended, brought up to date, but not quite the thing one knew and loved" ' (111). Strether must read between the lines that Madame de Vionnet has superscribed if he is to restore the text of Chad. But instead of saving meaning, he saves reading. The only booty he reaps from his adventure will send him reading to eternity, for he returns to Woollett armed with the complete works of Victor Hugo.

Strether's whole identity is intertextual. He oscillates between a reader and a book, because the novel systematically confuses reading with imagining. He shares the name of Balzac's novel *Louis Lambert*, and he can only certify his own existence through the mediation of the written word:

> His name on the green cover, where he had put it for Mrs. Newsome, expressed him doubtless just enough to make the world—the world as distinguished, both for more and for less, from Woollett—ask who he was. . . . He was Lambert Strether because he was on the cover, whereas it should have been, for anything like glory, that he was on the cover because he was Lambert Strether. (62)

The name makes the man. In effect, his reader is the author of his being. As editor, however, Strether half-creates each green instalment, and confounds the rôle of reader with the rôle of writer.

The second embassy stands for semantic, as well as moral, absolutism. Sarah condemns difference as fiercely as she censors sexual infractions. It is as if equivocation were a verbal form of fornication, and adultery a fleshly form of doubletalk. Strether tells her that she shuts her eyes to each side of the matter, 'in order, whichever side comes up, to get rid of the other' (279). For the sake of truth, she quashes otherness, and she seizes knowledge for the sake of domination. The many names for knowledge show that it is deeply in cahoots with power. To 'master' means to subjugate; to 'apprehend' means to arrest; one also speaks of 'grasping' meaning and of the 'possession' of the facts. Can truth be born without the violence of propriation? *The Ambassadors* pursues another form of truth, heterodox and volatile. Autocratic views of knowledge, pleasure, meaning and morality shudder under the effects of that which James calls Paris.

What is Paris? Paris 'is' nothing, for it names an energy within the text which dissipates identities and definitions. It designates a place, but it is inwardly displaced by the trans-Atlantic vacillations of its residents. A site of transformation, Paris is most itself when it is least itself, and passing towards a new, translated form of being:

> It hung before him this morning, the vast bright Babylon, like some huge iridescent object, a jewel brilliant and hard, in which parts were not to be discriminated nor differences comfortably

marked. It twinkled and trembled and melted together, and what seemed all surface one moment seemed all depth the next. (64)

This passage quivers like the city it describes, with 'signs and tokens . . . too thick for prompt discrimination' (120). For Paris is a text, and James's prose out-twinkles Babylon. Paris stands for the 'residuum of difference' in the text which eludes the wariest Pocock (21). The same traps that Paris lays for Strether trap the reader, too, for James mines his text with difference: 'Difference—difference from what he expected, difference in Chad, difference in everything; and the Difference, I also again say, is what I give.'[4] As soon as he arrives, Strether begins to sense 'the plenitude of his consciousness of difference' (60); and difference has the last word in the novel, too. He relinquishes Miss Gostrey and all the possibilities she represents to return to 'a great difference' (344)—and nothing more. In accepting Paris, Strether surrenders Mrs. Newsome and her world of things, identities and facts to a world of differences without positive terms.

As ambassador for Paris, Madame de Vionnet embodies 'the big Difference' (400; *N*, 412), and she unsettles the distinction between appearance and reality. She was, thinks Strether,

> like Cleopatra in the play, indeed various and multifold. She had aspects, characters, days, nights. . . . She was an obscure person, a muffled person one day, and a showy person, an uncovered person the next. (160)

All surface one moment and all depth the next, her power lies in her ability to differ from herself and to transform all those who surrender to the spell of her alterity. Into this welter of signification Woollett's representatives are dropped, on a mission to save Chad and single meaning.

Mrs. Newsome execrates the charms of difference. Strether identifies her with Queen Elizabeth, and the ruff that she engirdles round her neck represents the prohibitions stifling her ambassadors. He contrasts this 'frill' to the red ribbon that encircles Miss Gostrey's insurrectionary neck, altering 'the value of every other item' (42). For difference shimmers in her features, too, transfiguring their proportions. In the same way,

Woollett's fixities dissolve in Paris's mercurial morality. Once he has given his authority away (64), Strether learns to distrust Mrs. Newsome's 'fixed intensity' (248). 'She doesn't admit surprises', he complains:

> 'there's no room left; no margin, as it were, for any alteration. She's filled as full, packed as tight, as she'll hold, and if you try to get anything more or different either out or in—'
> 'You've got to make over altogether the woman herself?'
> 'What it comes to,' said Strether, 'is that you've got morally and intellectually to get rid of her.' [297–98]

Like Paris, Mrs. Newsome is a text, but her meanings and her morals waver as little as the gaze that she has fastened on Strether. Packed with positivities, she admits no revisions. 'She's the same', Strether realizes. 'She's more than ever the same' (343). To concede that vision is a 'process' (4) is to open the floodgates to alterity, so she prepares her conclusions before she has begun to probe the questions.

Difference, on the other hand, demands 'perpetual postponement' (390; *N*, 399). To read a text like Paris one must be prepared to wait for the charm of difference to emerge. The first paragraph of *The Ambassadors* hints of a 'secret principle' which enables Strether to 'wait without disappointment' (17); and he makes it clear to Sarah Pocock that waiting is an interpretive strategy. Chad's 'obscure', he says, 'and that's why I'm waiting' (192). The text is as dilatory as its hero: it practises what Barthes would call 'the infinite deferment of the signified'.[5] James recommends his reader to dawdle through the text as Strether ambles through his pilgrimage, for both must loiter and luxuriate in difference:

> Take, meanwhile pray, *The Ambassadors* very easily and gently: read five pages a day—be even as deliberate as that. . . . Keep along with it step by step—and then the full charm will come out. . . . I find that the very most difficult thing in the art of the novelist is to give the impression of the *real lapse of time, the quantity* of time, represented by our few poor phrases and pages, and all the drawing-out the reader can contribute helps a little perhaps the production of that spell.[6]

Woollett must have its meanings fast—as fast as it produces nameless articles. The Pococks could never cope with late

James. One can almost hear them muttering with Leavis that 'the energy of the "doing" (and the energy required for the reader)' are 'disproportionate to the issues' of the text; and Sarah would agree with Arnold Bennett that "the book was not *quite* worth the great trouble of reading it.'[7] James's prose refuses to save meaning. It wastes words and lavishes complexities, as if, in the textual economy, there were never any bills to pay. Rather than express the message, meanings twinkle, tremble, merge and deliquesce. By making Woollett an assembly line, James insinuates that bourgeois readings mimic bourgeois economics, to extort the highest profit from the text. Mrs. Newsome's interests lie in meaning, and she concerns herself only with the most efficient way to manufacture and recuperate it. Like Hegel's bondsman, a Woollett reader treats negativity as an investment which he cashes in for meaning in the end. But Strether resists the avarice of meaning. Like Hegel's lord who stakes his life, he knows that meaning is nothing but a moment in the play of negativity.[8] His 'only logic', therefore, is the logic of loss: 'Not, out of the whole affair, to have got anything for myself' (344). He squanders time and sense away till he has even lost himself in *jouissance*. Difference is 'only repeatable as difference', and Strether finds that to interpret the difference in Chad is to relive each lingering moment of his transformation.[9]

The Pococks must have answers. But *The Ambassadors* begins with a question, and the novel runs on questions as a machine runs on fuel. As the book proceeds, Strether surrenders his 'resolve to simplify' (162), and learns, instead, to draw a warm circle where every question 'would live . . . as nowhere else' (80). The 'most difficult of the questions' (102) has to do with the nature of the virtuous attachment, and it is also the only question which cannot be asked. The answer to Chad's enigma is sexuality, but it only manifests itself in silence and blanks, like Miss Barrace's 'Oh, oh, oh!' and little Bilham's 'Ah, ah, ah!' (124, 156–57, 160; 165). It was when Chad's letters stopped that his mother first suspected him of an irregularity, and his silence entices her to *read*. The Pococks penetrate this silence to reveal the secret shame beneath the dazzling show, for it was out of their forbidden union that the lovers wove their veil of reticence. But it is the change in

Chad's *appearance* that impresses Strether from the start. Thanks to the ministrations of his mistress, the outward show has triumphed over the dullest of realities. 'Tact' forbids Strether to denude the truth; tact sustains his questions as a lover procrastinates in his desire.

Tact is James's term for a certain code of discourse which avoids the vulgar truth but also steers clear of the vulgar falsehood. The forecourt Strether crosses to Madame de Vionnet's apartments is the architectural embodiment of tact, for James's houses tend to represent discursive strategies: 'large and open, full of revelations, for our friend, of the habit of privacy, the peace of intervals, the dignity of distances and approaches . . .' (145). To practise tact is to cultivate frank privacies and artless secrecies. As Chad puts it, 'I have no secret, though I may have secrets!' (142). The expression 'virtuous attachment' epitomizes tact, for it confounds the opposition between truth and falsehood. Appearance infiltrates reality, while truth and error flit like gleams and shadows in the jewel of Babylon.

'In the light of Paris,' little Bilham says, 'one sees what things resemble. That's what the light of Paris seems always to show' (126). Not what things *are*—leave that to the Pococks— but the metaphoric possibilities of things. In Paris, depth and surface coalesce, leaving nothing but the flux of figuration. Madame de Vionnet presides over a world of rhetorical as well as moral transformation, for she differs from herself in the same way that a metaphor daintily deranges definition. 'Memory and fancy couldn't help being enlisted for her' (318), Strether muses of the mistress of difference. 'She had taken all his categories by surprise' (161). The characters whom she refashions resemble metaphors themselves, for a trope is a rhetorical ambassador, hovering between two categories without contracting the Atlantic that gapes between. Strether speaks of 'embarking' on a simile as he would speak about embarking on an embassy (43). In the end, both errands lead him hopelessly astray.

2

As Mrs. Newsome's grip upon her representatives grows weaker, meanings drift as freely as ambassadors. Trope transfigures trope, and the signifier slips out of the clutches of the signified. The very notion of an origin grows thin and vague. For the light of Paris is the twilight of the idols, and truth a glimmer melting in the dusk. Set loose from Mrs. Newsome, the characters become ambassadors to one another; and power circulates among them, centreless and empty of intention. They think, act, speak and even desire on behalf of one another. As they relay each other's messages, instructions and requests, information buzzes round like power, destitute of origin.

Mrs. Newsome's power ebbs with every emigration. For she only needs to represent herself because she has already died a kind of death. As James writes in the Project for the novel:

> lively element as she is in the action, we deal with her presence and personality as an affirmed influence, only in their deputed, represented form; and nothing, of course, can be more artistically interesting than such a little problem as to make her always out of it, yet always *of* it, always absent, yet always felt. (379; *N*, 381)

Like God, Mrs. Newsome only manifests herself through scripture: her letters, which her ministers interpret according to their quota of imagination. Since these letters, too, are known in their deputed, represented form, the reader must concoct their contents. The text divulges only their effects and their trajectory, as they 'reckon with the Atlantic Ocean, the General Post Office, and the extravagant curve of the globe' (110).

Her missives, like her missionaries, spread the word of her existence, and her ambassadors function as human letters— texts incarnate—words made flesh. Although they are commissioned to extend her presence, they signify the emptiness at the origin of representation, in both its political and literary forms. Strether is thinking of that emptiness when he meditates that 'the main truth of everything was . . . that everything represented the substance of his loss . . .' (281).

Representation preys upon vacuity. Because he has missed life, Strether falls for the sorcery of reading, which is the repetition of another's writing. The pleasure of the text arises from the thrill of dispossession, too. An originary loss entices both the hero and the reader into a world of represented and vicarious delight.

James called his story a 'process of vision' (2), but a process of revision would have been an apter phrase, for deferred action structures both its form and content. 'Like the new edition of an old book that one has been fond of', the text re-reads the themes of *The American.* As the postscript prefaces the text, so the first time drops behind the second, and reading takes the place of the original experience. It is only through the medium of Strether's re-enactment that the reader can imagine Chad's seduction. And because the heir to Woollett screens himself with personal ambassadors, Strether meets the represented forms of Chad long before he encounters the original. On his first visit to Chad's home, little Bilham intercepts his gaze, and the two spies scrutinize each other. Little Bilham stands upon the balcony, blocking the window into Chad's domain, as if to intimate that representation abolishes transparency, occluding access to the signified. From the reader's point of view the text elides the whole encounter, for the second book draws abruptly to a close as soon as Strether has passed the *porte-cochère.* After a hiatus the incident is represented in the tranquillity of his chronically belated consciousness (70). The prose itself is missing its appointments with reality, so that it may represent the substance of their loss. When Strether takes the rôle of Chad and Chad begins to yearn towards Woollett, the second has usurped the first and representation has unseated presence.

Once the myth of the original dissolves, representation mimes representation and reality becomes a phantom hallucinated in the dying fumes of art. Strether treats his real adventure as a repetition of the 'images of his inward picture' (24). Life imitates imagination. 'It was the way of nine tenths of his current impressions to act as recalls of things imagined . . .' (172). The boundary melts that separates the theatre from reality, and the stage returns the gaze of its spectators: 'the figures and the faces of the stalls were interchangeable with those on the stage' (43).

It is in the theatre that Strether meets the altered Chad, who confuses the relationship between the subject and the object of the gaze. The rôles of watched and watcher oscillate throughout the text. Strether peers into Chad's 'private stage' in the hope of discovering a primal scene, but he is borne along instead by the compulsion to repeat it. Chad keeps his mother's agent under observation, too, often using little Bilham as binoculars (69). Surveillance is succeeding prohibition as the major strategy of power, because 'visibility is a trap', as Foucault says.[10] But who is framing whom within his vigilance? Mrs. Newsome only sees what her emissaries represent to her, so that the seat of power is the place of blindness rather than omniscience. Since there is no ultimate spectator, the world returns the viewer's stare. Other eye-beams cross the seer and the seen, and enmesh them in their subtle filaments. It is in the scene of Strether's last awakening that the gaze and the desire of the other shock him out of his phantasmagoria.

### 3

This scene occurs in Book Eleventh, where Strether's 'artless impulse' (301) to refresh his memory of Lambinet embroils him in the stratagems of art and love. Though difference has unshackled him from Mrs. Newsome and the despotism of identity, it conscripts him into other chains of power. His eye ensnares him in a new necessity, and frames him in its own picture-frame. Because every picture represents a loss, it functions as a trap to catch the gaze. It interpolates the seer in another syntax of desire, and the syntax of the prose re-enacts this drama of possession. In these two chapters the ruses of the words unmask the plots of power.

The chapter opens with the logic of loss. Strether is visiting the countryside in search of the Lambinet 'he *would* have bought' (301), but now concedes to nature. In his 'belated vision' (311), the present is already marked by loss and repetition, for the landscape represents its own unpurchased representation. Over and under the Lambinet other scenes and other arts twinkle and tremble together. The country is the 'nursery of letters' (301), as well as the nursery of trees, and its enchantments merge with those of painting, reading, writing and the theatre to create a semiotic landscape, or a language in green. However, the metaphors of art soon distort themselves into metaphors of artfulness, and words like 'fiction', 'fable' and 'performance' (311) come to mean the stratagems of guile rather than the visions of imagination.

Even the narrative is artful. For example, Strether basks in his remembered intimacy with Madame de Vionnet, and reflects that 'it was amazing what could still come up without reference to what was going on between them' (304). The text equivocates. Who are 'they', and what *is* going on between them? What, for that matter, is 'coming up'? Because the pronoun leaves the answer to the reader, he will combine the names of Chad, Madame de Vionnet and Strether according to his fantasy. Divested of their names, the characters may shed their stubborn positivity and circulate, so that the text hallucinates the intimacies it forbids. The syntax grafts Strether to the lovers and insinuates him into their desire.

By thinking of Madame de Vionnet, Strether is hollowing a gap out of the picture, for she is absent from its frame. At the same time, he ponders the abyss between them, and fancy, like 'a dismantled gate or a bridged gap' (24), reaches out across the void. Nonetheless, 'he really continued in the picture' (305), and he approaches an inn where he is told that two unexpected guests have just arrived in 'a boat of their own' (306). Like the *parerga* in a French landscape painting, these 'figures' float down the river to ornament the scene.[11] At the moment that they break into his vision, they also burst through his illusions, and even the chapter breaks to mark the rupture of the frame. Now, bespectacled as they may be, Strether's eyes perceived the fact of Chad's relation long ago, but the text suggests he must have 'scotomised' his own perception.[12] When he realizes that 'these figures, or something like them, had been wanted in the picture' (307), he knows that his vision all along has masked a lack. 'There is something whose absence can always be observed in a picture', hints Lacan.[13] What bursts through the picture-frame at last, like the return of the repressed, are the unbidden figures of sexuality.

109

It was in another picture that Lacan discerned the lack in vision, but it is also known as *The Ambassadors*. Two diplomatic figures stand on either side of Holbein's canvas, blankly returning the spectator's gaze. Around them appearances seduce the eye. But an impudent shape sneaks into the scopic field, perplexing the spectator who believes that he is master of the gaze. Hidden by a trick of perspective, this object only catches the spectator's eye when he begins to leave the painting's circle of enchantment. A death's head cuts across the foreground. Suddenly, the painting is revealed for what it is: a field of differences, lines of force, and vanishing traces. It is only by decentring himself that the spectator can complete the image, for this hidden skull opens a perspective which always takes the subject unawares.

The death's head winks back at the eye that ogles it. Like the veil of Parrhasios, the painting mimes the act of vision, rather than the world the eye beholds; it mimes the way that vision veils itself whenever it may catch the evil eye. Holbein's snide intruder hints that there is nothing underneath appearances but death. This is no ordinary death, but a death that coils around the living and burns its signature into the diaphane of the visible. Instead of seeing the whole picture, the spectator is overlooked by his own absence: 'Holbein makes visible for us something which is simply the subject as annihilated. . . .'[14]

James's *Ambassadors* reveals the lack in vision as the space of the desire of the other. In Holbein, skull and phallus merge, for death and sexuality combine to cicatrize the visible with lack. As Holbein's painting brandishes its artifice, so James's fiction broods upon its own devices. The text has taken in the reader much as the lovers have deluded Strether, for love and textuality are secretly in league and both are brutally exposed in their contrivances. The change from art to artfulness signifies a growing scopic scepticism, as the play of difference effaces the illusions of mimesis. Strether leaves Paris still believing that a picture represents reality, but by the time he returns he knows it is a net to trap desire. In the realm of desire, everyone is framed and no one sees the whole. Even Strether's eye can never take all pictures in at once. The lack in vision drives him 'from clever canvas to clever canvas'

(316), for every picture represents the substance of his loss. Between the picture and the subject it pretends to assuage, death inscribes its 'intimate difference' (394; *N*, 404).

## 4

*The Ambassadors* reveals that representation means the death of origins. In the realm of power the monarch is unseated by the very instruments of tyranny. 'A fantastic personage, at once archaic and monstrous', she sacrifices power in proportion to the power that she delegates.[15] Her letters supplement her living representatives, for deputation is a form of writing, as writing is a form of embassy. Both rebel. The play of difference unbinds the signifier from the despotism of the signified. 'With a deep audible gasp' Mrs. Newsome's fixities grow thin and tenuous (248). Her ambassadors invoke her phantom to justify their own belatedness, but in effect the representative begets its origin. For no one would have ever dreamed of any brooding omnipresence of the law except to vindicate the presence of its representatives.

Strether leaves Woollett as the 'long arm' of the law, deputed to reflect the sovereign as the moon reflects the sun (396; *N*, 407). But he stumbles into a wonderland of negativity. Mrs. Newsome fades into a nervous memory, and the authority of the original disintegrates in a kaleidoscope of difference. However, the convulsions of the old régime bring forth a stranger form of power, too inhuman to be lodged in the person of the sovereign. This power infiltrates through pleasure, rather than repression. It interpolates the subject in a field of forces, like a switchboard that nobody controls. All experience becomes vicarious, for everyone is captured in the labyrinths of another's being. The gaze interpenetrates them all.

The realm of vision has its own theocracy. Either the seer rules the visible and circumscribes the world within his gaze, or else the visible enslaves the seer to its own priority. Though they seem to be opposed, these two perspectives endorse each other; for whether they assert a sovereign subject or a sovereign object, they do not question sovereignty itself. *The Ambassadors* shows that 'the seer and the visible reciprocate one another and we no longer know which sees and which is seen', as Merleau-Ponty writes.[16] Moreover, every picture has a gap where the seer may be seized in the gaze and the desire of the other. Gazes cross and interweave; for a gaze refers to other gazes as a word refers to other words, and as a force refers to other powers. It is their negativity that lends them their identity, but also means that each must differ intimately from itself. As the hero of the novel, Strether surrenders his identity to difference, too, for he forfeits all he might have called his own for a 'supersensual hour' in the pleasure of the other (379; *N*, 228). 'Yes,' writes James, 'he goes back other, and to other things' (403; *N*, 415).

NOTES

1. Jacques Lacan, *The Four Fundamental Concepts of Psycho-Analysis*, trans. Alan Sheridan (London: Hogarth, 1977), p. 112.
2. James described the novel as a '*supplement* of situation' in his Preface, which was itself a supplement, having been written six or seven years after the novel itself. See *The Ambassadors*, ed. S. P. Rosenbaum (New York: Norton, 1964), p. 3. All page references in text are to this edition.
3. See Michel Foucault, *The History of Sexuality: An Introduction*, trans. Robert Hurley (London: Allen Lane, 1978), especially pp. 88–98.
4. In the case of Notebook entries and the 'Project of Novel by Henry James', page references to the Norton edition are followed by the corresponding page numbers in *The Notebooks of Henry James*, ed. F. O. Matthiessen and Kenneth B. Murdoch (New York: Oxford University Press, 1961), designated by *N*: in this case 389; *N*, 397.
5. Roland Barthes, *Image—Music—Text*, ed. Stephen Heath (Glasgow: Fontana, 1977), p. 158.
6. 408; also in *Selected Letters of Henry James*, ed. Leon Edel (London: Rupert Hart Davis, 1964), p. 225.
7. 438; rpt. from F. R. Leavis, *The Great Tradition* (New York: New York University Press, 1963), p. 161; for Bennett, see *Henry James: The Critical Heritage*, ed. Roger Gard (London: Routledge & Kegan Paul; New York: Barnes and Noble, 1968), p. 373.
8. See Hegel, *The Phenomenology of Spirit*, trans. James Bailey (London: Allen and Unwin; New York: Humanities Press, 1931), pp. 228–40. See also Jacques Derrida, 'From Restricted to General Economy: A Hegelianism without Reserve', in *Writing and Difference*, trans. Alan Bass (London: Routledge & Kegan Paul, 1978), pp. 251–77.

9. Barthes, p. 159.
10. Foucault, *Discipline and Punish*, trans. Alan Sheridan (London: Allen Lane, 1977), p. 200.
11. See Derrida, *La vérité en peinture* (Paris: Flammarion, 1978), especially Ch. 2.
12. See Freud, 'Fetishism', in *On Sexuality*, the Pelican Freud Library, Vol. 7 (Harmondsworth: Penguin, 1977), p. 353.
13. Lacan, p. 108.
14. Lacan, p. 88.
15. Foucault, 'Prison Talk', in *Power/Knowledge: Selected Interviews and Other Writings 1972–1977*, ed. Colin Gordon (Brighton: Harvester, 1980), p. 39.
16. Maurice Merleau-Ponty, *The Visible and the Invisible*, trans. Alphonso Lingis (Evanston: Northwestern University Press, 1968), p. 139.

# 6

# Representing the Author: Henry James, Intellectual Property and the Work of Writing[1]

## by STUART CULVER

In 1934, more than twenty-five years after the publication of
the New York Edition, R. P. Blackmur collected Henry
James's prefaces in *The Art of the Novel* and introduced the
volume as 'the most eloquent and original piece of literary
criticism in existence'.[2] The prefaces, Blackmur believed, offer
more than practical criticism of the texts by the man
responsible for them; James is concerned also to define this
responsibility, his 'artistic consciousness', to describe how he
participated in the production of his works and what sort of
authority he continues to exercise over them.

Readers of the Edition, however, have disagreed about the
nature of the author James portrays, a disagreement reflected
in the different responses to the prefaces by two of the
novelist's closest friends, Edmund Gosse and Percy Lubbock.
Lubbock was convinced that James regarded these introductory comments as a platform for articulating a theory of
composition; rightly read, Lubbock thought, the prefaces
constituted a how-to manual which explained to the apprentice exactly how in each case the Master got his job of
representing done. James's commentary, however, does not

rehearse the rules of fiction systematically enough, and Lubbock found it necessary to supplement the prefaces with his own study, *The Craft of Fiction* (1921), the book most responsible for establishing James as an advocate of objective representation, of 'showing' instead of 'telling'.[3] The trouble with the prefaces for Lubbock was that the novelist compromised his manual by paying too much attention to the personal reminiscences evoked by each work. Gosse, on the other hand, found the essays 'disappointing' precisely because they paid too much attention to technique and not enough to reminiscence; though the novelist, Gosse believed, promised to 'take us, with eyes unbandaged, into the inmost sanctum of his soul', the results are 'dry, remote and impersonal'.[4]

At stake in these divergent readings are two very different notions of what an author is and what sort of work he does. Lubbock saw James as the master craftsman of fiction, the writer most conscious of the techniques available and most rigorous in applying them. Lubbock's 'author' is an artisan wholly absorbed in the process of fashioning an object that will, when finished, stand independent of him. Crucial for Lubbock is the craftsman's impersonality; in the well-made fiction, the subject dictates the work of composition, and the author disappears in order to let the subject appear more completely. Gosse, conversely, understands the author's labour as the antithesis of craft; on his view, James is something like an intuitive genius whose memoirs are of interest insofar as they reveal how the accidents and contingencies of his private life resulted in just these texts. Fiction is for Gosse essentially a personal achievement dependent on the unique constitution of the autonomous creative soul.

Questions about the author are, of course, central to any collected edition. Who ought to appear in such a form? Who counts as having a corpus? What does it mean for an author to have become such a canonical figure? Are we to read such authors differently? The answers the prefaces provide to these questions are unavoidably conditioned by the kind of collected edition they introduce. The New York Edition is, after all, a luxury item and not a scholarly edition of James. The novelist published his works in this format to capitalize on the popularity of a particular kind of publishing commodity; the

115

de luxe edition, which flourished on the subscription market from 1880 to 1910, presented the complete works of noted authors in expensive, ornately-bound and lavishly-illustrated volumes. These collections were as much a sign of the era's interest in bric-à-brac as a reflection of changing critical standards; yet the very possibility of such a commodity indicates how closely the popular conception of authorship was allied to that imagined by Gosse. In the eyes of its purchasers, the de luxe edition conferred celebrity status on certain cultural heroes, and the 'works' of such public figures as Lincoln and Theodore Roosevelt appeared in this form.[5] As a rule these sets were limited in number in an effort to accentuate their claim to embody each celebrity's unique self. On this popular view, the obligatory prefatory remarks, provided by the author exclusively for this edition, authenticated the volumes with the force of an autograph, reassuring the buyer that this was in fact a relic of the great man.

Lubbock saw the Edition's value in entirely different terms. James's collection functioned, he thought, as a resource for the would-be writer, offering both a series of well-made, exemplary artifacts and explanatory comments. Lubbock's apprentice reads the Edition to learn the Master's trade secrets, notably his technique of limiting point of view to the third person centre of consciousness. The prefaces, according to Lubbock, foreground this technical device which simultaneously objectifies the novelist's authority and 'pushes his responsibility further and further from himself'. The Jamesian centre distinguishes the man from his work, and so Lubbock's 'lesson of the Master' is exactly the negation of the de luxe edition's value: 'This is not *my* story, says the author; you know nothing of me' (Lubbock, 147).

In the prefaces James describes the author's authority over his work in terms of another kind of labour, one more securely placed in the general economy. In an extended metaphor the novelist identifies the author with the civil engineer:

> He places, after an earnest survey, the piers of his bridge—he has at last sounded deep enough, heaven knows, for their brave position; yet the bridge spans the stream, after the fact, in apparently complete independence of these properties . . . and the rueful builder, passing under it, sees figures and hears

116

sounds above: he makes out, with his heart in his throat that it bears and is positively being 'used.' (*AN*, 297)

One could see in this figure two alternative accounts of the literary text's commercial value. On the one hand, there is a labour value of the builder's work (the time, effort and material the bridge cost); on the other, the bridge's exchange value (its worth in the eyes of those who use it in their daily commerce). But the text is defined here as a public work, a means of conveyance, and the civil engineer exercises a peculiar authority over his products, one that escapes the contradiction between labour and exchange value and complicates the distinction between Gosse's autonomous creative soul and Lubbock's craftsman. A public servant who oversees a communal enterprise, the engineer does not own the bridge he builds, but sells his expertise for a fee.

Bridges and other crucial public works must be guaranteed, and civil engineers, guardians of technological expertise, were among the first occupational groups to organize themselves as a profession. The British Institute of Civil Engineering was formed as early as 1818, and by the middle of the century the apparatus of the self-regulating profession was largely in place—there were schools, journals and an ethic of public service. In America, engineers first organized themselves on a regional basis: groups like New York's American Society of Civil Engineers (1852) and Boston's Society of Civil Engineers (1848) included, along with practising engineers, amateurs with only a passing interest in questions of technology. By 1867, however, the New York-based A.S.C.E. began to extend its influence geographically and to regulate professional activity more thoroughly. In 1895 membership was restricted to those capable of designing machinery or public works. The success of this organizational program depended on features unique to the work of engineering; it required mastery over an esoteric body of knowledge and commitment to an ethic of public service—that is, to the perfection of the task for its own sake, indifferent to questions of profit and economy.[6]

Together with the physician, the civil engineer occupied an exemplary position among nineteenth-century workers. Professionalization restructured the engineer's place in society by insisting that his practice was both too crucial and too complex to be left subject to the vagaries of the marketplace. The autonomy of professional practice appealed to other occupations; the client could only accede to the professional's superior knowledge and authority. But this autonomy was not premised on an inborn talent or gift unique to the individual practitioner; rather, it depended on his or her affiliation and education, a process of accreditation and training that elided the distinction between self and skill by completely reforming the individual's thought processes. The professional's commodity was really only a habit of mind or expertise, and it was the responsibility of the professional organization to oversee the production of its practitioners, to license its members and so regulate their practice. The profession accomplished this in alliance with the university, the site where the professional self was fashioned. The engineering curriculum was designed to ground the future bridge-builder's expertise in a theoretical knowledge base; the student's familiarity with the laws of calculus and physics exceeded any conceivable practical necessity if only to make science's neutrality and rationality a habit of mind. Unlike the craftsman, the professional was not trained on the job by the example and advice of fellow workers. Education was now in the hands of specialists, taking place in the classroom and laboratory, removed from the place of work and from practical considerations. At the same time, through its liberal arts courses, social organizations and sports, the university imparted an ethos and moulded the professional character. In this way the university education obscured any clear distinction between the autonomous self and professional expertise. The career afterwards similarly combined public with private as the vita recorded both social and professional accomplishments in a pattern that frustrated any effort to distinguish the individual from his or her work.[7]

Precisely because professional expertise inhered in the practitioner's self, the exchange between expert and client could not be treated as just another commercial transaction. Neither the engineer nor the physician left behind a tangible product that the client could evaluate. Ultimately only one's peers were capable of judging professional practice and then only with the discourse of the discipline itself. For just these reasons the profession defined its 'commodity' as the performance of a service and not the manufacture of a product. In the consultation the client purchased for a time the practitioner's 'self'. The professional exchange therefore differed ethically from the sale of the craftsman's artifact (Larsen, 56–63).

Burton Bledstein has argued that the 'culture of professionalism' infected the aspirations of many nineteenth-century occupations; plumbers and undertakers sought to secure their respective places in the general economy by insisting that they too performed a public service grounded in esoteric knowledge and requiring autonomy in practice (Bledstein, 36). Authors too were attracted to the professional model and invoked its ideology in discussions of literature's function in society. In *Pen and Book* (1899) Walter Besant, founder of Britain's Society of Authors, noted the ability of the contemporary man of letters to 'command an income and a position quite equal to those of the average lawyer or doctor'. Besant thought that this status both well-deserved and necessary for a public servant whose job it was to diffuse 'modern sympathy'.[8] Arnold Bennett, in *How to Become an Author* (1903), described the author's new-found status in different terms; the modern author, he suggested, had more dignity simply because so many people were now willing and able to buy his wares.[9] Bennet was, nonetheless, a member of Besant's Society.

In his effort to organize writers Besant invoked some features of the professional model, but his Society of Authors was not truly a professional organization. Underlying the Society's formation was the state of affairs in the literary marketplace emphasized by Bennett; literature, fiction in particular, represented an increasing portion of the G.N.P. This involved more than the advent of the mass-produced best seller. The years between 1880 and 1910 saw a proliferation of print media: little magazines appeared along with dime novels; de luxe editions, along with illustrated newspapers. With the recognition of international copyright and the protection of the author's rights over his or her texts' translation and dramatization, it became evident that existing contracts between publishers and authors were quickly becoming obsolete. The

Society of Authors served really as a clearing-house for information on the mechanics of publication and the nature of the author's property rights in his text. The organization lobbied for reforms in contracts and extensions of copyright legislation that would recognize more completely the author's ownership of his text.[10]

The Society believed that the authorial profession would only be secure when society as a whole recognized writing as a form of making and the text as the author's private property. Literary property, the organization's monographs declared, involved a special kind of ownership; the literary text was more inalienable, more proximate to its maker than other artifacts: 'Property means a man's very own, and there is nothing more his own than the thought created, made out of no material thing.'[11] This argument collapses the distinction between Lubbock's craftsman and Gosse's creative genius in order to emphasize the common presupposition that literary work is a form of making unlike other kinds of manufacture, which depend inevitably on tools and materials from outside the person. Bennett is more willing to identify writing with mass production: 'Any author who knows his craft can easily . . . compose three thousand words of his very best in a week' (Bennett, 26). But Bennett's position is really no different from Besant's; the independence both claim for the author depends on making, producing a commodity with a market value. Both want the author to profit as much as possible from the sales of his or her text.

The authors' emphasis on private property and manufacture contradicts professional ideology. The purpose of distinguishing service from commodity was to escape just the market value Besant's Society embraced; the service, that is, is not an artifact and has no real exchange value. Instead the professional is indirectly remunerated, paid a fee fixed by the community of practitioners. The profession 'owns' collectively the right to practise certain skills, to apply the knowledge that is produced within the community by the discourse of its members. The civil engineer participates in projects too large and too undeniably public to allow any claims of private ownership. For the profession, then, intellectual property is not the right to one's product; rather, it is the right to practise in the first place—belonging to the group that has a monopoly over certain practices and skills.

The Society of Authors, I want to argue here, misunderstood the conception of intellectual property underlying copyright legislation and its enforcement in both England and America. The first copyright statute, the Act for the Encouragement of Learning (1709), was designed essentially to protect the investments of publishers by securing their monopolies over the texts they issued. The author's property rights came about by accident, as a means of ensuring that book-making would be a profitable enterprise and of policing the manufacture of literature. The same gesture that acknowledged the author's rights in his work qualified his authority over it; the text could (and can) only be copyrighted after it has been signed over to a publisher and transformed into a purchasable commodity.[12] The American copyright statute was more consciously conceived as a strategy for ensuring the production of books and the circulation of ideas. The Constitution grants Congress the power 'to promote the Progress of Science and the Useful Arts, by securing for limited Times to Authors and Inventors the exclusive Rights to their respective Writings and Discoveries' (Article I, section 8, number 8). Madison defended this authority, arguing that 'the public good fully coincides in both cases with the claim of the individual.'[13] A property right is invested in the author simply to encourage literary production; recognizing that the nation needed its authors but lacked institutions to patronize them, Madison assumed that the best way to encourage writing and to guarantee the means of communication was to allow authors to treat their texts as property and so profit from their sales.

The Society of Authors, nevertheless, argued, that as important as copyright legislation was, the written laws finally failed to take fully into account the inalienability of literary property. The authors thought the statutes merely institutional supplements to a more profound right over the text: 'What a man produced by his brain was by Common Law his own forever.'[14] As late as 1890 the Society made this claim, but by 1834 both British and American courts had dismissed this common law right. In that year the American Supreme Court reviewed the case of Wheaton versus Peters; the question at issue was whether or not the author who had failed correctly to register his copyright had any recourse in the courts for its infringement. The court found that he did not, agreeing with the earlier British decision in Donaldson versus Becket (1774).

The policy of both legal systems was to give the statute 'a liberal construction in order to give effect to what may be considered the inherent right of an author in his work'.[15] But this made little difference when an oversight in the registration effectively erased all claims over the text. The legal rights over the work instituted by copyright supplanted all other rights, redefining the writer's authority as something other than a common-law property right in the work of his brain. Copyright, a limited and conditional monopoly over a sequence of signs, remunerated the writer's service indirectly by granting him or her proprietorship over a stretch of public domain—language and ideas—in the belief that a nation could best secure its means of communication by turning pieces of it over to individuals who then became responsible for overseeing its circulation. There are obvious affinities between the legal notion of copyright and the profession's definition of intellectual property; the text, like the bridge, is a means of conveyance, a public work, and the author's job is to maintain the flow of words and ideas. But, even if the author's property right is a secondary phenomenon, it nonetheless differentiates writing from true professional service by leaving the writer in an entrepreneurial rôle, concerned with the market value of a particular commodity.

When James invokes the civil engineer as a model for the author he remains aware of the difference between the two kinds of work. For James, the analogy serves ultimately to underscore a crisis in the author's authority: 'the bridge that spans the stream' does so 'after the fact' and 'in apparently complete independence' of the author's expert design. James's 'rueful builder' is anxiously aware of a gap between span and support, but, nonetheless, finds himself taking credit for an enterprise in which he did not quite participate and for which he would rather not, it seems, be responsible. If the span holds, commerce goes on undisturbed, and the author is not exposed as the charlatan he actually is. If James's author resembles the engineer by ensuring the means of communication, his authority is dangerously compromised and involves an element of amateurism and speculation.

Though they invoke the professional model, the prefaces, then, acknowledge its essential distance from literary authority. James's essays are really most clearly aligned with professionalism in their parody of the how-to manuals of Besant and Bennett. Despite his claim that the prefaces would 'form a sort of comprehensive manual or *vademecum* for aspirants in our arduous profession', James offers little or no practical advice on how to conduct the business of writing, where to send manuscripts, in what form, etc.—questions that occupied both Besant and Bennett. In fact the scene of writing described by the prefaces is too reduced and too immediate to allow any comprehensive account of the conditions of literary production. We are given only glimpses of the author at work, partial views more arbitrary than systematic. Though the novelist remarks that 'a living work of art, however limited, pretends always, as for part of its grace, to some good faith of community, however indirect, with its period and place', he trivializes this 'community' past significance when he worries whether the rickety table on which he is forced to write will have any deleterious effects on the formal balance of the works composed on it (*AN*, viii, 213, 218). James is able only to render the work of composition within the close confines of his work-room. Typical is his Bolton Street apartment where many of the Edition's works were composed: a 'great house' obstructs his view of Picadilly, and, he remarks 'opposite my open-eyed windows, it gloomed, in dusky brick, as the extent of my view, but with a vast convenient neutrality' (*AN*, 212). The world outside has taken on the form of the blank page in front of the working writer. The 'vast convenient neutrality' of the opposing wall may suggest the author's independence from his world, but the emphasis throughout the prefaces is on the marginal relationship of author to world, not on his complete independence. Invariably for James the trivial, superficial circumstances prove the ones most necessary to the actual work of composition; consistently the prefaces make marginal conditions appear central. In a way the tendency is the same one at work in all his later fictions; the outside world impinges on the scene all the more sharply for having been so reductively presented.

The preface to *Roderick Hudson*, which introduces the Edition as a whole, raises the same question about what counts as the 'author' but from exactly the opposite perspective. As the novelist begins his glance back over the body of his work, too many associations are evoked, and he is unable to determine which of these memories were essential to the productive process. James compares the prefacer's situation to that of an archaeologist reading 'a recording scroll or engraved commemorative table', not because the signs are alien or obscure but, rather, because there are too many possible meanings and he must choose uncertainly among them. The first preface thus questions directly James's ability to define his artistic consciousness—to determine, that is, which aspects of his past experience count as part of the work of writing. All the while, in the process of re-reading, the distinction between public and private selves 'quite insists on dropping out' (*AN*, 4). The novelist in a later preface describes the threat posed by this chaos of reminiscence in a striking image:

> The shrunken concomitants muster again as I turn the pages. They lurk between my lines; these serve for them as the barred seraglio-windows behind which . . . forms indistinguishable move and peer. (*AN*, 125)

The page itself is a tangle of associations which threatens ultimately to flood the text, turning the print itself into margin.

The way to contain this flood of reminiscence, James suggests, is to keep always in mind a critical sense of one's subject. But no *a priori* definition of authorship is available, and the prefacer must rely instead on a continually revised reflection on the particular definition as it has unfolded so far. He must assume somewhere 'a visibly-appointed stopping-place', a distinction to be drawn between those aspects of his life involved in artistic production and those essentially private. But, with no theory of the author, the prefacer 'is condemned forever and all anxiously to study' his past work, while 'the veiled face of his Muse' remains hidden and no absolute separation of man from author is possible (*AN*, 3). The ability to isolate the authorial self depends finally on a professional faculty essential to all representation, 'the honest sense of life', which is simultaneously the prefaces' subject (the artistic consciousness) and the means for discovering that subject. But this sense is disturbingly unconscious,

> fed at every pore even as the birds of the air are fed; with more and more to give, in turn, as a consequence and quite by the same law that governs the responsive affection of a kindly used animal, in proportion as more and more is confidently asked. (*AN*, 201)

This crucial talent, strangely alien to the prefacer, is, he suggests, like a domesticated animal whose productive capacities have been so highly developed that it has become in effect a machine.

Contrary to Lubbock's argument, James does not use the prefaces to justify his favourite compositional strategies or to ground them in a theory of what writing ought to be; rather, he discusses them as his 'inveterate habits'. His practice has become so thoroughly ingrained that it is now second nature. William James defined habit similarly in his *Psychology*; it is the slippage of once-conscious, chosen actions into unconscious, automatic behaviour.[16] Like the professional, the author has developed a skill inhering in his self. Once so professionalized, the author (or his work) can no longer be represented. His work no longer distinct from his person, 'all we then—in his triumph—see of the charm-compeller is the back he turns to us as he bends over his work' (*AN*, 96).

What *can* be represented is the 'amateur', 'the artist deluded, diverted, frustrated or vanquished' (*AN*, 97). The subject of the prefaces becomes this amateur, who, by being so acutely aware of what he is about, is all the more uncertain which is the right way to proceed. If the prefaces parody the manual by insisting that the author's skill is unrepresentable, they also reject that professional model by finding their subject in the amateurism inevitable in the work of writing—an authority, like that of the 'rueful' bridge-builder, dangerously compromised.

James insists on the author's amateurism not to set fiction apart from commerce, but, conversely, to demonstrate more clearly how his authority is conditioned by the commodity status of his texts. Advances in the technologies of reproduction and marketing similarly compelled the courts to reconsider what an author was and how aesthetic value operated in the marketplace. In the case of Bleistein versus Donaldson Lithograph (1898) a Federal District Court ruled that the advertising poster could not be copyrighted; the poster, however beautiful, was designed, Justice Evans contended, specifically 'to lure men to a circus' and was, therefore, 'merely frivolous, and to some extent immoral in tendency'. His ruling is rooted obviously in several commonplaces about what counts as artistic labour. The poster is not subject to copyright, Evans holds, because its maker has already been paid and because his labour was from the outset contaminated by extrinsic, commercial motives. The judge defines art strictly in terms of the object's relationship to the marketplace; the moral force of his decision is energized by his belief that art ought to be pure, disinterested and noncommercial labour (*Decisions*, 270).

Four years later the Supreme Court overturned Evans's ruling. Oliver Wendell Holmes delivered the majority opinion, arguing that an object does not have aesthetic value simply because it stands outside commercial exchange. Holmes suggested that the object counts as a work of art (and can be copyrighted) only if it has a certain intrinsic value: 'A very modest grade of art has in it something irreducible, which is one man's alone. That something he may copyright' (*Decisions*, 278). At the same time that aesthetic value is, for Holmes, intrinsic to the artifact, it is also, he thinks, tenuous and needs protection from the fluctuations of the marketplace. The author's conditional monopoly over his text works to foster and preserve this 'irreducible' 'something'. Yet Holmes can only define this ineffable, intrinsic value in terms of the marketplace; we know that this 'something' is in Bleistein's poster simply because so many people are willing to buy copies of it; and 'the taste of any public', Holmes believes, 'is not to be treated with contempt.' Holmes has, in effect, defended the vulgar taste: it's art, that is, if the people say it is. Aesthetic value, on this view, is not outside the economy but thoroughly implicated in it, and it is speculation itself that the court protects with copyright. Bleistein, as an artist, is granted the privilege to profit again and excessively from his mercenary work. Aesthetic value is just this inexplicable, excessive demand; the 'rush' or 'boom' is both evidence that a given artifact is art and the service that artists provide. As Holmes puts it, the 'real use' of the work of art may be 'to increase trade and help make money' (*Decisions*, 279).

Art cannot be completely professionalized as long as its 'product' is popular assent itself. The lesson of Bleistein versus Donaldson Lithograph is that artists are always amateurs and speculators, if only because literary property is not the ownership of a quality put into the work by its maker but the right to create value by publishing and republishing the text. The writer's authority is entrepreneurial. Though he may regard himself as a public servant, the author must find his wages in his commodity's exchange value, and, as Holmes suggests, his work of marketing the text is finally what counts as his public service. This argument leaves the writer suspended between the two model figures discussed thus far; neither a maker nor a professional, he is both closely involved in commercial exchange and concerned more with managing than manufacturing. In an effort to master this contradiction the prefaces turn to another model, a figure just then emerging in industrial society, the shop manager or mechanical engineer, whose job it was to oversee the increasingly complex machinery of mass production. Like the author, the manager was both entrepreneur and professional.

The growth of industry and the mechanization of productive processes required more sophisticated approaches to management, and Fredrick Winslow Taylor responded with a campaign to redefine it as a science. The aim of Scientific Management, or Taylorism, was to develop a managerial strategy that could prevent strikes, eliminate 'shirking' by workers and maximize production by applying scientific principles to business practice, rationalizing production through time and motion studies and more rigorously defining the worker's task through studies of physiology and psychology. This restructuring of work processes depended on the gaze of the scientist, who stood apart from the productive process itself. Unlike the world of craft, where the practitioner knew best his own practice, in Taylor's factory, labour functioned best when least conscious and most completely mechanized. Taylor's manager dissects his workers' bodies into a set of marketable skills or muscular capacities, defining their respective 'individualities' as what remain outside the work process, what they do after work.[17] At a ball-bearing factory where Taylorism was employed, the women who inspected the finished product were tested to determine their hand-eye co-ordination; those with too low a 'personal co-efficient' were dismissed

> And unfortunately this involved laying off many of the most intelligent, hardest working, and most trustworthy girls because they did not possess the quality of quick perception followed by quick action. (Taylor, 90)

The worker's 'character' was not a variable in the efficiency expert's calculations.

Imbalances in the economy were for Taylor only accidents to be managed away by a more systematic organization of the work force. He never questioned the public's capacity to consume and continued to insist that unrestrained production, absolute efficiency, was the name of the manufacturer's game:

> Whenever an American workman plays baseball, or an English workman plays cricket, it is safe to say that he strains every muscle to secure victory for his side. He does his best to make the largest number of runs. (Taylor, 13)

Thorstein Veblen, in *The Engineers and the Price System*, argues that Taylor addresses only one side of industrial 'sabotage' by failing to challenge industry's financial managers—investment bankers whose 'conscientious withdrawal of efficiency' maximizes profit at the expense of unrestrained production.[18] Profit, Veblen thinks, supplants both human needs for the product and the innate desire to score as many points as possible. What disturbs Veblen most about this scandal is that ultimate control over industry is in the hands of 'amateurs' unfamiliar with technology and speculating on the very imbalances of supply and demand Taylor wanted to manage away. Veblen, like Taylor, would hand the factory over to its professionals, the mechanical engineers, who understand its inner workings and want only to increase production without concern for the market value of the product themselves.

The managerial scene depicted in the prefaces tells a some-what different story about the production of a Jamesian text. Though James takes up Scientific Management's division between labour and management, he rejects its valorization of unrestrained production. The prefaces actually parody the cult of efficiency underlying Taylorism by emphasizing the author's inability to regulate his own unconscious productive processes and insisting on the inescapability of Veblen's 'financial management'.

For James, 'in art economy is always beauty', but this 'sublime economy' of representation poses a managerial prob-lem. The work of composition is a 'modern alchemy' that transforms life's 'splendid waste' into 'the most princely of incomes' by isolating 'a hard latent value' in the midst of seemingly valueless elements. Life, on this view, is a mean-ingless, unrestrained productive process which threatens, through over-production, to overwhelm and elide all differ-ences and values. The novelist's alchemy is really a strong form of reading; he must 'make out' his subject (the value he wants to preserve) 'on the crabbed page of life' and disengage it 'from the more or less Gothic text in which it has been placed' (*AN*, 120, 63). While his subject on rare occasions appears to James already complete, a 'suddenly-determined *absolute* of perception', more frequently it comes to him as a wind-blown 'germ' that stirs his imagination 'as at the prick of some sharp point' (*AN*, 151, 119). Once so noted, detached from life and appropriated for fiction, the germ is deposited in the novelist's imagination, the soil in which it takes root. The germ grows all unconsciously as it dwells in the imagination in association with other notes taken and germs picked up; until, by the force of its own growth or in response to an editor's call, it emerges. Now the author appears as the Master, a 'weird harvester' whose crop resembles all too closely life's 'splendid waste' as it bears more fruit than the harvester can manage. He must cut back desperately in an effort to regulate a productive process that bewilders him and constantly exceeds his control as he struggles to fashion a publishable commodity and a hard latent value out of his imagination's free play. The Master in this scenario is uncannily like Chaplin's worker in *Modern Times*, overwhelmed by the machinery of mass-production, a consummate amateur (*AN*, 312).

Composition in the prefaces appears as a form of over-seeing, a managerial relationship between author and subject more volatile than that described by Lubbock. The precariousness of the Master's authority is most clearly expressed in James's transition from plant to animal imagery. If the germ begins as a seed planted in the imagination's soil, it emerges as an animal with a will of its own, making the work of management all the more difficult:

> Once "out", like a house-dog of a temperament above con-finement, it defies the mere whistle, it roams, it hunts, it seeks out and "sees" life; it can be brought back but by the hand and then only to take its futile thrashing. (*AN*, 144).

The subject remains incompletely domesticated, and the violence of punishment serves only to remind the Master that he has merely a conditional command over his trainee.

Yet James actively cultivates this compromising position. The 'energy' of his art, he believes, 'fairly depends on his fallibility', his inability to master the process of imagination. The prefaces articulate an aesthetics of difficulty, presup-posing that 'whatever makes' the job of writing 'arduous, makes it, for our refreshment, infinite' (*AN*, 297, 3). The appeal of the short story form for James is precisely the difficulty of containing one's imagination of the subject within such close, arbitrary limits; the author must turn '. . . the whole coach and pair in the contracted court, without the "spill" of a single passenger or the derangement of a single parcel' (*AN*, 179). This spectacle of skill is premised on the novelist's having gotten himself all amateurishly into a tight place only to display his ingenuity and thrill his audience. James's professional author stages his own amateurism to invest the compositional process with the 'thrill of a game of difficulty breathlessly played' (*AN*, 311). The notion of sportsmanship at work here differs importantly from Taylor's; while Taylor is interested only in offensive production, the Jamesian player writes himself into a corner to stage a resourceful escape and recoup a mastery he has willingly compromised.

The techniques James foregrounds in the prefaces, his

'inveterate habits', all contribute to this perverse management of the formal economy. Foreshortening, scenic presentation and the centre of consciousness are strategies for staging this managerial crisis within the form. The most general of these favoured techniques, foreshortening, is explicitly defined as a way 'to give all the sense, in a word, without all the substance or all the surface' by enforcing a distinction between what is essential to the subject and what is only marginal. The novelist does not disguise this difference; rather he insists that his conscientious withdrawal of efficiency, his compromise, makes his art 'exquisite' and 'repudiates the coarse industries that masquerade in its name' (*AN*, 14).

The Jamesian centre is typically viewed as an outgrowth of the novelist's epistemology—his 'modern' belief that knowledge is subjective—but the prefaces are more concerned with the economic advantages of this approach to point of view. The centre allows the Master simultaneously to manage the flow of representational values and to insure their precariousness, to stage the managerial crisis and to represent the author's relationship to his text.[19] At one point James insists that his agent is always only obliquely involved in the story; 'more or less detached' from the subject *per se*, the centre 'contributes to the case a certain amount of criticism and interpretation'. But this oblique access to the subject proves paradoxically the most direct approach to its value; the indirectly involved appreciator, James believes, offers the only way 'not to betray, to cheapen, or, as we say, give away, the value and beauty of the thing'. The resort to an agent within the text is not a means for grasping the subject itself more completely but for making it accrue value. Authority is displaced to capitalize on the gap between sense and substance and so to inflate the subject's value: 'the affair of the painter is not the immediate, it is the reflected field of life, the realm not of application but of appreciation' (*AN*, 327, 67, 65).

This inflation is by no means easily controlled. Hyacinth Robinson, who serves along with Fleda Vetch as the prototypical Jamesian centre, is bewildered by the play of conflicting values (James tells us there can be no story without bewilderment). Hyacinth is able only to appreciate those values without mastering them. Inflation goes unchecked and the centre succumbs:

> He collapses, poor Hyacinth, like a thief at night, overcharged with treasures of reflection and spoils of passion of which he can give, in his poverty and obscurity, no honest account. (*AN*, 156)

Hyacinth could steal more than he could legitimately take in; thus he fails to manage the economy within the story that it is his job to manage for the author and his readers outside. The Jamesian point of view is not then, as Lubbock would have it, a technique for closing off the text's play of values or containing their fluctuation. It is really just the opposite: a strategy within the text for conscientiously withdrawing efficiency, for both staging and acknowledging that the work of composition is essentially a matter of financial management, amateurish speculation.

The prefaces, as I read them, use the language of financial management to describe the work of composition and so recast the author's rôle in the scene of writing. But this interpretation raises two distinct questions: what are the consequences of this understanding of composition for James's actual financial practice? and what difference does this argument make for our conception of James as the Master?

The project of prefacing in general recasts the writer's authority. We are now familiar with the argument that prefaces necessarily recast our sense of the text's closure and self-sufficiency, thereby revising our beliefs about how language represents. The very fact that something remains to be said reminds us that the fictional representation is by no means definitive. Further, it suggests that there is a difference between the author's intention (to render his subject completely) and the text itself, which requires the supplement of authorial commentary to close its case. The gesture by which the author acknowledges responsibility for a compromised authority over his representation contaminates all levels of the text with the difference felt between intention and language, signifier and signified. But, for James, what is most important in prefacing is the division within the authorial self; as his own reader, the writer takes up the work of his own hands as if it were another's. The New York Edition revises and repackages works that had already circulated, and, in it, James exploits the labour of a prior, now-alien self producing nothing new except the prefaces themselves.

The editorial rôle James must play collapses the distinction between financial management as a compositional resource and as a commercial strategy. The author is essentially an entrepreneur reasserting his property rights over his texts by recasting their published forms, making them circulate again as new commodities while leaving them substantially (and legally) the same. The Master, therefore, is parasitic on work already done, a reputation already made and productive processes now alien to him. He is not, as both Lubbock and Gosse assume, a maker at the height of his powers. He is as bewildered by his own work as Hyacinth is by the world around him. His authority is by no means absolute; he differs from the reader not because he is more familiar with the genesis of his texts but, rather, because he exercises his legal privilege to over-see their circulation, to place them in a new commercial context.

What is finally at stake here is the ontology of the literary work. In the collected edition, the text's value is redefined as the reader's focus shifts. The individual text, now a member of a set of works (a corpus), is inscribed in a network of cross-references, anticipations and repetitions, which restructures its 'intrinsic' value. Moreover, a second edition, it now must be read in reference to its own prior manifestations. On this view, the effect of the definitive edition, especially when compiled by the author, is really to make definitiveness and stability impossible for each included text. The author can no longer be called an artificer simply because his texts are no longer fixed verbal constructs. His authority is now modelled on the managerial power invested in him by copyright law; he exercises a reserve of rights to over-see and speculate on the texts' dissemination in various forms, a reserve produced by (predicated on) the texts' appearances as commodities circulating beyond his immediate control. Authority as defined by copyright is displaced and conditional—exploitative yet limited in time and by law, violent yet insecure. The New York Edition, I want to suggest, is a peculiar commercial venture which offered James an opportunity to express how the text's fate as a commodity re-wrote his own rôle as its author and at the same time altered the operation of aesthetic values in society.

If I am right and the prefaces address the symbiotic relationship between the writer's authority and his property rights, then we need to read these essays as something more than documents of formalist aesthetics. We need also to re-evaluate the rôle of the Edition in the novelist's biography. The standard account of James's later career associates his failure on the stage and subsequent retreat from London to Rye with the professional decision to practise pure art, to dwell as it were only in the unconditioned 'country of the blue'. The late style, the title 'Master', the unserialized last novels, all are taken as evidence of James's rejection of the literary marketplace. Even in a book concerned explicitly with the novelist's implication in the mass market, Marcia Jacobson regards the Edition and its prefaces as basically anti-commercial; in contrast to the early, pre-theatre James who wanted to be 'a spokesman for his whole culture', the 'persona of the New York Edition's prefaces', she believes, 'is that of James the Master, an aloof, self-sustained artist' for whom fiction 'is a vocation undertaken in the service of the author himself'.[20]

In the argument I am advancing here, the prefaces expressly dismiss this portrait of the Master in order to describe a more complex authority that is thoroughly implicated in the literary marketplace and in no way 'self-sustained'. James's later career, I think, represents a series of strategies for realizing this new understanding of authorship as management; on my view, the novelist's late style is inseparable from his new practice of composition by dictation and revision; the Jamesian centre is implicated in the same logic of mastery that led the novelist to employ a literary agent; and all of these strategies recognize the model of the author—and of the text's ontology—engendered by copyright statutes and the changing technologies of the literary marketplace.[21] James, in his later phase, was, if anything, more concerned with how literature functioned in the general economy. His prefaces acknowledge the commercial situation of all literary production and attempt to master it by re-defining the author as the seat of displaced, conditional powers over the text's dissemination, an authority grounded in the surrender of any claims to private property in the work of one's hands.

## NOTES

1. Walter Benn Michaels read and commented on earlier versions of this essay, and I am greatly indebted to his criticism. Three essays have influenced my approach to the prefaces: Philip Fisher, 'Pins, A Table, Works of Art' in *Representations* 1 (February 1983), 43–57; Michel Foucault, 'What is an Author?' in *Textual Strategies*, ed. Josué V. Harari (Ithaca, 1979), pp. 141–60; and Walter Benn Michaels, 'The Man of Business as a Man of Letters' in *American Realism: New Essays*, ed. Eric Sundquist (Baltimore, 1982), pp. 278–95.
2. Henry James, *The Art of the Novel*, ed. R. P. Blackmur (New York, 1934).
3. Percy Lubbock, *The Craft of Fiction* (1921; rpt. New York, 1957).
4. Edmund Gosse, 'Henry James' in *Scribner's* 57 (April and May 1920), 422–30 and 548–57, p. 422.
5. See discussions of these editions in Charles Madison, *Book Publishing in America* (New York, 1966) and Raymond Kilgour, *Estes and Lauriat: A History* (Ann Arbor, 1957).
6. Daniel Harvey Calhoun, *The American Civil Engineer, Origins and Conflict* (Cambridge, Mass., 1960) and Edwin T. Layton, *The Revolt of the Engineers* (Cleveland, 1971).
7. My account of professionalism is based largely on Magali Sarfatti Larsen's *The Rise of Professionalism* (Berkeley, 1977) and Burton Bledstein's *The Culture of Professionalism* (New York, 1976).
8. Walter Besant, *Pen and Book* (London, 1899).
9. Arnold Bennett, *How to Become an Author: A Practical Guide* (1903, rpt. New York, 1975), p. 10.
10. The history of the Society of Authors is recounted in Victor Bonham-Carter, *Authors By Profession* (Los Altos, Ca., 1978). But see also John Goode, 'The Decadent Writer as Producer' in *Decadence and the 1890s*, ed. Ian Fletcher (London, 1979), pp. 109–30.
11. The Society of Authors published several monographs on this issue, most notably John Lely's *Copyright Law Reform* (London, 1891). This remark, however, comes from a publisher, R. R. Bowker, writing in George Haven Putnam's *The Question of Copyright* (New York, 1891), a volume which supported the authors' demand for extended rights over the text.
12. See Lyman Patterson, *Copyright in Historical Perspective* (Nashville, 1971) for a complete discussion of this debate.

13. *The Federalist*, Number 43 (1788; rpt. New York, 1961), 271–72.

14. S. Squire Sprigge, *The Methods of Publication* (London, 1890), p. 12.

15. *Decisions of the United States Courts Involving Copyright and Literary Property*, ed. Wilma S. Davis (Washington, D.C., 1980), Myers versus Callaghan.

16. William James, *The Principles of Psychology* (1890; rpt. New York, 1950), pp. 104–27.

17. Frederick Winslow Taylor, *The Principles of Scientific Management* (New York, 1911).

18. Thorstein Veblen, *The Engineers and the Price System* (New York, 1921).

19. Laurence Holland was the first critic of James to treat the centre of consciousness as a representation of the writer's authority and his implication in his story. See *The Expense of Vision* (1964); rpt. Baltimore, 1980).

20. Marcia Jacobson, *Henry James and the Mass Market* (Birmingham, Alabama, 1983), pp. 6, 1, 19. Throughout her study Jacobson opposes 'vocation' to 'business', believing that James wanted finally to recoup an authority compromised by the commodification of literature. My belief is that the commodity status of his texts provided James with a model for his authority.

21. In a recent article on the New York Edition, Michael Anesko argues that the enterprise was essentially commercial; James, he thinks, gave up his plans to make the collection an artistic whole, surrendering to the exigencies of the market. This argument, however, continues to distinguish artistic work (and aesthetic value) from commercialism. My point here is that the Edition and its prefaces insist that these two orders of values are fundamentally the same and that the Edition represents not the abdication of authority but its definition in terms of the commercial system. Cf. Anesko, ' "Friction with the Market": The publication of Henry James's New York Edition' in *N.E.Q.* 56 (September 1983), 354–81.

# 7

# James as Janus: Opposition and Economy

## by ELLMAN CRASNOW

'Beginnings, as we all know, are usually small things',[1] wrote
Henry James; but he could at least draw on a larger rhetoric
than ours. One useful figure that seems to have lapsed is that
of invocation. James could write 'Oh, spirit of Maupassant,
come to my aid!'—or, on less exalted occasions, '*À moi*, Scribe;
*à moi*, Sardou, *à moi*, Dennery!'[2] This is such a comforting
manoeuvre that I propose to reintroduce it. I invoke a god; I
call upon Janus. As the god of doorways and gates, he is the
god of beginnings, and so proper to my setting-out.[3] Indeed,
his monument in the Forum seems to have been used for
ceremonial beginnings: as, for example the setting out of an
army in proper form. The monument was kept open in time of
war, and 'closed only in the rare event of universal peace'. I
see in all this a Janus who presides over spatial and symbolic
*division*: a god who distinguishes between inside and outside, or
between other sets of opposites. But it is not a simple binarism.
The open door, the possibility of passing through, suggest a
subversion of opposites, a transgression of separate realms.
This view of Janus would push him closer to the rôle of
Hermes as boundary-crosser[4]; and it suggests the method that
I shall use in this study of some of James's writing. There is,
however, another and perhaps more common received image
of Janus: 'When represented otherwise than by the gate, his
symbol was a double-faced head, a very old art-type, sometimes

awkwardly joined to a body.' If I am right and this is now the more common view, it is interesting that the common view seems to have endorsed a simple binarism, in which the doorway's chance of transit and transgression gives way to the fixed alternatives of the double gaze. This latter is the unproblematic, pre-reflective Janus, and I propose to move from him towards the problematic version, from the naïve towards the sentimental in Schiller's terms. And not only in Schiller's terms. I shall be interested in writings where subjective sentiment abounds, in contrast to James's more objective ideals.

Janus was credited as the source of various kinds of knowledge, among them the idea of coinage. That is to say, Janus founds the exchange of symbolic tokens of value; he must be credited (credited!) with the institution of a monetary economy. This 'economy' of Janus suggests two further usages. When James wants a totalizing model of the writing process, he repeatedly refers to an economy; and the term is also used by Freud to describe functional models of the circulation and distribution of psychic energy.[5] I propose in what follows to attempt a functional insight into the economy of certain Jamesian texts.

Think of joining James and Janus, the Master and the god. James would certainly have relished the ritual pre-eminence; as god of beginnings, Janus headed all lists, outranking even Jupiter. And as a connoisseur of form, James would have approved the link with a god of proper form. This becomes still stronger when we think of James in the framework of fictional theory; he has been most widely used as a source of formal criteria. These criteria are established, in part, by means of an oppositional structure inscribed in James's work: anecdote versus picture, form versus substance, figure versus character, and so on. It was this prevalence of oppositions that suggested the use of Janus to trace an underlying economy in James's non-fictional work, rather than repeat the formal categories that have already been so amply described.

The clumsy phrase 'non-fictional work' suggests another concern. His formal eminence has meant that we read James's non-fiction very selectively, unevenly and unfairly. How much skipping, for example, goes on in reading the Prefaces to the New York Edition—where, in order to find our formal nuggets of ficelles and foreshortening, of character and consciousness, we have to sift through a detritus of digressions (as they appear to us) on circumstance and origin. The embarrassment is even greater in the *Notebooks*, with their sentimental exhortations and abnegations. The line of least resistance is to treat all this as a kind of autobiography—but then if we look at James's own autobiographical practice, we find the other side of this clipped coin, an obverse impurity; for here it is theoretical and conceptual matter—discussions of imagination, of representation and memory—which loop away from linear narrative.

It thus appears possible to read some of James's *own* works as 'loose baggy monsters'[6]—to quote his own description of *War and Peace*. Monstrosity is always interesting; in myth, it often seems to stem from transgression as miscegenation—that is, from mixtures of the wrong *genus* or kind; for our purposes, we might say from mixtures of genre.[7] This suggests that we may be misreading James in terms of a naïve Janus, in terms of a simplistic opposition between, say, 'criticism' and 'auto-biography', and that we need to transgress this division. That is to say, we need to relate his works to a more fundamental economy than that of genre. But how are we to arrive at this economy? What interests, what motive forces are involved?

A formal analysis might suggest itself. But if we define formalism as a study of the autonomous aesthetic object, then there is a deep irony in James's status as a formalist hero. His theorizing is emphatically linked to questions of creativity and inspiration—hence the difficulty of reading the Prefaces, as described above. His is an aesthetic economy geared to production. But this production has within it a conflict of values which it will be my main purpose to explore. I can anticipate it briefly by describing James's problematic in terms of two views of the material of artistic production. The first view sees material as a means: as the object of an active acquisition, accumulation and transformation. The second sees material as an end, and as the subject of a largely passive solicitude; if action is involved, it should be celebratory rather than transformative.

This is not a new form of aesthetic anxiety. One aspect, its fear of detachment, is focused through the thematic guilt of the nineteenth-century 'palace of art'—as in Tennyson's poem of that name, or as quoted in *The Golden Bowl* or in *A Small Boy and Others*, where it is significantly juxtaposed with 'the house of life'.[8] But if James's problematic is not original, his exploration and exposition are unusually illuminating, and lend themselves to the method of Janus; that is to say, to the development of a series of oppositions which are subject to the permeability of their division, to passage in and out through the symbolic door.

The first set of oppositions relies precisely on motions in and out seen in aesthetic terms; I refer to the concepts of impression and expression, both widely used by James. 'Impression' is indeed one of his favourite terms. It is for us a half-forgotten metaphor; but if we look back into its metaphoric function, we find that it posits a pliant matrix, something that is stamped or sealed, something that receives the imprint. The subject position of impressionism is on this reading typically passive; and the economy of impressionism involves receiving and keeping, acquisition and accumulation. These processes are highly valued in James. The 'Art of Fiction' essay ranks 'a capacity for receiving straight impressions' above the possession of taste, as far as aspiring novelists are concerned.[9] In *Notes of a Son and Brother* the narrator recalls offering himself as 'a plate for impressions to play on at their will'; elsewhere, he haunts the Palais Royal

> as if to store up, for all the world, treasures of impression that might be gnawed, in seasons or places of want, like winter pears or a squirrel's hoard of nuts, and so perhaps keep one alive. . . .[10]

This is accumulation with a vengeance. But the ideal, the solipsistic simplicity of this one-way traffic is elsewhere insufficient for James. To what continuum does the atomistic impression relate? Can it be regarded as experience, or as knowledge?[11] At one stage, an exclusive impressionism—exclusive through being too narrowly occupied with an unreflective sensuality—is seen as subject to Promethean punishment, gnawed by a vulture on its back.[12] Impressions, then, are not self-validating. Nor are they innocuous in their accumulation; on the contrary, they can multiply to the point of threat, becoming 'a deep-down jungle of impressions that were somehow challenges'.[13] Now this last extract displays a typical shift of agency; the impression as challenge, unlike the impression as treasure, is almost animate. And elsewhere it is wholly animate: 'They had begun, the impressions—that was what was the matter with them—to scratch quite audibly at the door of liberation, of extension, of projection. . . .'[14] It is dangerously easy to dismiss this sort of passage as mere decorative figuration. What it does is to reverse the direction of impressionist theory; for once impression is projected outwards—that is to say, expressed—its vivid subjective immediacy is compromised. Representation is a deferment, and narrated impression is belated impression. The 1905 essay on Balzac glances at this point by reference to the lyric poet who speaks 'from his individual heart, which throbs under the impression of life', and who is contrasted with the kind of writer who 'has begun to collect anecdotes, to tell stories, to represent scenes', and who consequently 'is well on the way not to be the Poet pure and simple'.[15] Whether or not the romantic immediacy of this 'poet pure and simple' sounds plausible does not concern us here; what is at issue is the reversal, from impression to expression.

Now one way of viewing impressionism sees its subjective passivity as rendering it unfit for expressive activity, as making it likely to prove weak in execution and organization. There is, to be fair, an alternative view which sees impressionism as freed for advance in execution and technique through its break with literal representation.[16] But the young Henry James, like many early critics,[17] held the former view. He wrote of the impressionists at the 1876 exhibition that they

> abjure virtue altogether, and declare that a subject which has been crudely chosen shall be loosely treated. They send detail to the dogs and concentrate themselves on general expression. Some of their generalizations of expression are in a high degree curious.[18]

Two years later, writing about Whistler in the *Nation*, he returns to the attack: 'It may be good to be an impressionist, but I should say on this evidence that it were vastly better to be an expressionist.'[19] The contrast makes a nice cheap journalistic point for James, but we have seen that his own critical practice undermines it; impression already involves expression. And expression, for its part, can be seen as necessarily involving the prior interiority of impression—else what would there be to express? The direction, of course, is reversed, and we now *begin* with what Derrida calls 'the expulsion of the intimacy of an inside'.[20] Put like this, expression appears as a kind of Fall, an expulsion from Edenic intimacy; and we shall indeed find a certain prelapsarian nostalgia later on.

In terms of its imaginative economy, expressionism does seem to differ from impressionism, since production is involved by definition, and thus the subject is active—whereas impressionism could *appear* passive. But the activity of expressionism raises the question of creative deformation, of doing violence to the material. Both impression and expression can be accused on the grounds of 'treatment'; and for both, the concept of realism becomes hopelessly problematic.

To sum up what has been said so far, and to point the way forward, I want to cite a famous passage from *A Small Boy and Others*—so famous, indeed, that as John Pilling complains, it has rather obscured the rest of the book.[21] It is what the narrator calls 'the most appalling yet most admirable nightmare of my life'[22]—the dream of an assault and a repulse, set in the Galerie d'Apollon at the Louvre. It is embedded in a chapter which begins with an account of the overwhelming cultural impression of Paris, a Paris where the very houses seem to say 'Yes, small staring jeune homme, we are dignity and memory and measure', and the rue de Seine utters darkly 'Art, art, art, don't you see? Learn, little gaping pilgrims, what *that* is!' All this is only a prelude to the revelations of the Louvre, and in particular to 'that bridge over to Style constituted by the wondrous Galerie d'Apollon, drawn out for me as a long but assured initiation'. There is now a chronological jump from this early experience of the palace of art to the nightmare, which took place much later. Interestingly, the account begins when the pursued has already become the pursuer; the dreamer chases a dim figure, as he says,

142

out of the room I had a moment before been desperately, and all the more abjectly, defending by the push of my shoulder against hard pressure on lock and bar from the other side.

The dreamer *forces the door outward* and routs his assailant:

he sped for *his* life, while a great storm of thunder and lightning played through the deep embrasures of high windows at the right. The lightning that revealed the retreat revealed also the wondrous place and, by the same amazing play, my young imaginative life in it of long before, the sense of which, deep within me, had kept it whole, preserved it to this thrilling use; for what in the world were the deep embrasures and the so polished floor but those of the Galerie d'Apollon of my childhood?

The whole passage is a perfect illustration of what Freud says in *The Interpretation of Dreams* about contrariety and reversal; it is also relevant to the theme of melodrama explored by Peter Brooks[23]; but of course what interests me is: who gets through the door? The symbolic site of Janus is evident: a problematic spatial division between inside and outside, the inside under threat from the outside in a manner that recalls the challenging jungle of impressions. Here it is Paris as cultural monument that offers the immediate challenge; more generally, we can think of any pressure on an imaginative economy to absorb and react. The successful shift from passivity (or passive resistance) to active response leads to mastery of the monumental site. The Galerie, previously figured as a tube or tunnel for the ceremony of initiation, is now a backdrop for the fugitive's dimly diminishing figure.

What this account leaves out are the feelings that the passage invokes, the truly melodramatic emotionalism with which it is imbued. The emotion is so great as to be called sublime: 'the sublimity . . . of the crisis had consisted of the great thought that I, in my appalled state, was probably still more appalling than the awful agent. . . .' 'Sublimity' may do justice to the scale of the emotions, but not to their awkward and even contradictory moral implications. For once the tables are turned the values shift; the assailant is now 'dismayed', while it is the protagonist who displays 'straight aggression and dire intention'. Hence the assailant becomes, at least

143

potentially, a pitiable figure; readers of James's fiction will recall that this effect is fully realized in the story of 'The Jolly Corner', which uses a similar reversal.

We are dealing with a structure of apparent oppositions: passivity and activity, inside and outside. By making the dream into a drama of reversal, a chiasmic crossing, the oppositions can be maintained, the double gaze of Janus undisturbed. We then produce an aesthetic fable along the lines of Wallace Stevens' 'violence from within that protects us from a violence without'.[24] The trouble with this account is that, as we have seen, the violence will not stay abstract and fixed, but involves a moral problem which may add turpitude to the protagonist's triumph; he is, potentially, guilty.

And it is precisely a potential guilt which pervades the critical writing. We are all familiar with those moral dilemmas in James's fiction which render relations suspect because relation seems always liable to slide into exploitation. Hence the withdrawals, the sacrifices and the expiations that have been so widely noted. But the whole problem can be and is transposed into James's non-fiction, where it provokes an elaborate rhetoric of passivity and solicitude.[25] It is as if the economy of literary production has been invaded by an ecology party voicing accusations about exploiting the material, depleting the resources and despoiling the environment. In this economy, simple unchecked consumption belongs to an innocent past (and here we may think of Proust); this past is figured in the *Autobiography* as a 'vast succulent cornucopia' which belonged to a 'more bucolic age of the American world'; as the narrator recalls,

> We ate everything in those days by the bushel and the barrel, as from stores that were infinite; we handled water-melons as freely as cocoanuts, and the amount of stomach-ache involved was negligible in the general Eden-like consciousness.

James's adult economy is, by contrast, much concerned with budgeting, and above all concerned with quality rather than quantity—with quality, that is, as attributed to the material. For the material figures not just as an object for consumption by the self, but as an other in relation to the self; and relation, as we have seen, may be exploitative.

Of course this is most marked in the discussion of character; but it is part of the rhetoric that *any* entity, through reification and personification, can achieve character-status and be treated as such. It then becomes, in *its* turn, a subject: that which, as its root *sub-jectum* implies, may be 'thrown under' or subjected by the power of the other.[27] The other in this instance is the subject of writing, as distinct from the newly dignified subject of representation. The power-relationship between these two can be expressed in overtly political terms:

> It all comes back, in fine, to that respect for the liberty of the subject which I should be willing to name as *the* great sign of the painter of the first order. Such a witness to the human comedy fairly holds his breath for fear of arresting or diverting that natural license. . . .[28]

This appeal to liberty and natural law still suggests a fairly abstract linkage; but another rhetoric of relationship expresses itself in emotive and even erotic terms. There is a progression, as expressed in the Preface to *The Princess Casamassima*, from 'observation' through 'reflection' and 'appreciation' to a felt 'appeal' and a claimed 'intimacy'.[29] The solicitude of the writing subject is matched in a solicitation by the represented subjects, who 'hover' and 'flush' and 'throb' in recurrent appeals for existence. Now the guilty activity of writing *is* permissible, since it is only a response to an appeal, a giving-in, and can in that sense be evaluated as 'passive'. It is a matter of appearing to delimit the activity of creative intention. James sometimes describes creative process in chemical or alchemical terms, 'the mystic process of the crucible',[30] that prefigure T. S. Eliot's impersonal catalyst in 'Tradition and the Individual Talent'; but his key term in this area is 'surrender'; and surrender, of course, precisely inverts the power-relationship of the two subjects, though it need not cancel their eroticism. Thus at one point in the *Notebooks*, when the advantages of a new subject appear, James writes 'Porphyro grows faint really as he thinks of them.'[31] The Keatsian intertext of 'The Eve of St. Agnes', with Porphyro as lover and voyeur, is peculiarly illustrative of this attitude to subject-matter.

There is a more sober statement of surrender in the late

essay 'On Consciousness and Immortality' where, speaking of the artist, James says 'of him is it superlatively true that he knows the aggression as of infinite numbers of modes of being'; and, again, 'the artist's surrender to invasive floods is accordingly nine-tenths of the matter that makes his consciousness.'[32] This passage seems to approach the limits of passive rhetoric. Aggression and invasion suggest an influx that may be threatening rather than appealing, and return us to the problems of the Galerie d'Apollon. The problem of action and violence—or, rather, action *as* violence—is again familiar through James's fiction, and its themes of victimage and vampirism. As a reminder, I quote an early and lurid formulation by James's amanuensis Theodora Bosanquet:

> When he walked out of the refuge of his study into the world and looked about him, he saw a place of torment, where creatures of prey perpetually thrust their claws into the quivering flesh of the doomed, defenseless children of light.[33]

Of course, this is quite unlike the home life of our own dear author; Bosanquet emphasizes that such things were strictly confined to the fiction. Now biography is not my concern; but as regards criticism, I am intrigued to find the narrator of the Prefaces explaining that 'with the longest and firmest prongs of consciousness, I grasp and hold the throbbing subject.'[34] In this and in many other instances (particularly in a series of images of penetration), one finds already inscribed in James's criticism an active aggression that counterpoints its passive guilt. Thus Leon Edel's contrast between active art and passive behaviour[35] is inadequate; the art encompasses both passivity and activity. Its 'throbbing subject' can be a fictive entity, an external stimulus, or a memory trace, as in this strange passage from the Preface to *What Maisie Knew*:

> at a simple touch an old latent and dormant impression, a buried germ, implanted by experience and then forgotten, flashes to the surface as a fish, with a single 'squirm', rises to the baited hook, and there meets instantly the vivifying ray.[36]

This grotesquerie appears to me not accidental, but symptomatic of the heterogeneous ideas here yoked by violence together. The impression is at first a 'dormant' and 'implanted' 'germ'—that is to say, agency is organically displaced. The

146

'simple touch' appears as accidental, but it is also meta-morphic; the germ becomes a 'fish' and, newly animated, rises to the 'baited hook' which figures as some sort of conscious intention—and rather cruelly so, because fish that are hooked usually die, and this fish has after all just begun to live. But of course it need not worry; the 'vivifying ray' of aesthetic salvation is already at hand. The ray seems somehow comic; perhaps it is a piece of fugitive science fiction from H. G. Wells, still at that stage James's friend; but its rôle in what has now become a moral economy is evident.

Where there is a more single and assured theoretical position, the comedy is more stable. Here, for example, is an unashamedly activist argument, demolishing the claims of passive reproduction as they are embodied in an anonymous critic of the 'slice of life' school:

> you may again and again see him [i.e., the critic] assist with avidity at the attempt of the slice of life to butter itself thick. Its explanation that it is a slice of life and pretends to be nothing else figures for us, say, while we watch, the jam superadded to the butter. For since the jam, on this system, descends upon our desert, in its form of manna, from quite another heaven than the heaven of method, the mere demonstration of its agreeable presence is alone sufficient to hint at our more than one chance of being supernaturally fed.

All this is very comforting, but 'the phenomenon is too uncanny' to be believed. The loaf of life has had to be sliced, method and selection have had to intervene, and there is no really amorphous subject:

> Let it lie as lumpish as it will. . . . it has been tainted from too far back with the hard liability to form, and thus carries in its very breast the hapless contradiction of its sturdy claim to have none.[37]

Form thus informs the formless, helped by the urbane formal extension of James's late style.

We do not see this selective activity as malign—our moral imagination is not, after all, exercised over a loaf. But selection means exclusion, and insofar as material is given inherent value, just so far may exclusion arouse anxiety. The opposition that then appears is one of form versus content; and the most extreme version I know is in James's *Theatricals*, unacted plays published in the '90s and prefaced with what is referred to as 'melancholy subterfuge',[38] a strained mixture of prescription and consolation. The activity of selection is here particularly cruel because exercised through 'that bitter humiliation . . . the inexorable, the managerial "cut" '—personified as 'the foul fiend Excision', and Miltonically dignified as 'the blind Fury with th'abhorred shears'.[39] This activity threatens to turn the plenum of representation into a void—or, as James writes, 'the vessel is not in proper trim till she is despoiled of everything that might have appeared to make her worth saving.'[40] Nevertheless, it appears that just such a drastically stringent selection allows a specially intense residuum to survive, something like the essence of dramatic form; or, as James puts it, 'There is no room in a play for the play itself until everything (including the play . . .) has been completely eliminated.'[41]

This may serve as James's version of *l'absente de tous bouquets*. It is no doubt a piece of special pleading; but there are plenty of other arguments for ferocious activity, for selection or for the drive to 'Convert, convert, convert!'[42] and for the tendency to patronize what is called 'the thing of accident' as 'mere actuality, still unappropriated'.[43] If we recall Derrida's point about propriation as the process which organizes symbolic exchange in general,[44] it is evident that we have returned to the question of an economy, whose exchanges may now be clearer. It is very much a question of propriation and exchange, rather than of settled property. The active and passive drives (with all their transformations) constitute and support each other in an interdependent circulation. The self cannot be purely passive; it needs an other, if only for definition. To posit the other is an activity; but the other, once posited, is a potential source of concern which must be allayed by recourse to passive values, which in turn qualify the activity; and so on. Nietzsche would have been horrified by such a model[45]; but it does seem to apply. And model-building as such, the very concept of a structure of balances and compensations, suits the desire for determinate form which is described by James precisely in terms of architecture and building.[46] Yet on the other hand it seems *in*appropriate to his flights of extravagance and emotion, to that sublimity which, as Longinus claims, leads to a transport beyond the bounded self, beyond a closed economy. How can we resolve this difference?

The word 'economy', according to Marc Shell, 'refers etymologically to the conventions (*nomoi*) of and distribution (*nemesis*) within the household (*oikos*).'[47] *Oikos, nemesis* and *nomoi* together produce *oikonomia*, economy. Economy is thus etymologically speaking an artifice, a custom and convention, belonging to the realm of *nomos*. But I have previously cited that attitude to character which involved 'respect for the liberty of the subject' and 'natural license'. To speak of natural license or natural law is to reject mere human convention and to appeal to the way things 'really' are, to the realm of *physis*. Or, to put it another way: the two faces of Janus now appear as those of nature versus culture, a *topos* which recurs in Classical, Renaissance and Romantic thought. It is the eternal task of conservatives to argue for a 'natural' economy, but etymologically speaking this is a contradiction in terms. And of course it is also a problem for aesthetics. The way out—or, rather, the way through the door—has typically been by way of organicism. Organic form is seen as nature's own convention—the *nomos* of *physis*, as it were—and thus as closing the gap between the two terms. Thus we can read in the Prefaces that 'I delight in a deep-breathing economy and an organic form'[48]—a nice juxtaposition, in which the convention or artifice of economy is naturalized by the epithet 'deep-breathing' and so made fit for organic company. Much of the discussion of active and passive drives could be rephrased in organic terms; as, for example, describing the artist's sensibility as 'the soil out of which his subject springs',[49] and thus transforming creative activity into a passively enabling environment for growth, an aesthetic compost if not manure.

Organicist metaphor is, of course, a rephrasing and not a resolution. Strictly speaking, the legitimations of nature are unavailable to culture, as Jonathan Culler and others have shown.[50] Yet there is a loose sense of organic form which does point to a difference from the internal dispositions implied by 'architecture'. This form is 'organic' simply by contrast with what is seen as mechanically controlled; thus digressive

instead of progressive, subjective instead of objective, display-
ing its own dynamic as if it were a principle of growth. Now
this is the last sort of thing that one usually associates with
James's reputation as a stylist, and yet his non-fiction is
full of it. We tend to deprecate the mode because James
deprecates it: '. . . these are wanton lapses and impossible
excursions; irrelevant strayings of the pen, in defiance of
every economy.'[51] Such reproaches, however, do not prevent
the proliferation of 'lapses': of exhortation, resolution, reminiscence, anticipation. These lapses feed into what I would
offer as the great Jamesian countertext, that other practice of
writing which the brilliance of his novels has made us neglect.
The most suitable name for this countertext is 'scenario'. This
is a term usually applied to the plans for future works which
James dictated to his typists. Now while these plans do, in
different degrees, offer examples of the writing to which I refer,
it is not confined to them. I would extend the scenario mode to
include passages in the *Notebooks*, the travel writings, the
Prefaces, and above all the late masterpieces of autobiography.

The scenario functions as both pretext and metatext, in that
its topic is, recurrently, another writing which it both engen-
ders (hence its organicism) and proleptically describes. It
manages to transgress most of James's rules and to subvert
most of his oppositions—'the practice of the discursive well-
nigh overmastering its principle',[52] as we read in *Notes of a Son
and Brother*. Perhaps the most striking of these transgressions is
the first person intrusion, the loss of detachment, the surrender
to what James called 'that accurst autobiographic form which
puts a premium on the loose, the improvised, the cheap and
easy', and which involved 'the terrible *fluidity* of self-revela-
tion'.[53] 'Fluidity' and looseness together suggest a certain
concern for the definition of self, an anxiety over boundary and
identity. We have already glanced at oppositions of self and
other in the active/passive opposition; it is a problem that
does not seem nearly so acute in the scenario. I suspect that
this is because the scenario is always, to a degree, reflexive; the
writing subject surveys its own transformation through ana-
lepsis or prolepsis. This sounds narcissistic, and indeed Freud's
1914 paper on narcissism is *à propos*; it points out that the
narcissistic person may love what he (or she) is, what he was,

what he would like to be, or someone who was once part of himself[54]; and all of these transformations are available in the autobiographic scenario. The first person may multiply and shift, as in these notebook extracts planning the story called 'The Next Time':

> *I* become the narrator, either impersonally or in my unnamed, unspecified personality. . . . I seem to catch hold of the tail of a glimpse of my own personality. I am a critic who doesn't sell, i.e., whose writing is too good—attracts no attention whatever. . . . I am the *blighting* critic. . . . She wants me to praise her, so that THAT may help her not to sell. But I *can't*—so sell she does. I think I may call the thing *The Next Time*.[55]

Notice the final shift from an enunciated to an enunciating subject. The 'I' of this text consciously does double duty, and that is its interest. Elsewhere in the *Notebooks* we read of 'the double consciousness, the representation of which makes the thrill and the curiosity of the affair, the consciousness of being the other and yet himself also. . . .'[56] The scenario self, then, is its own other—as of course the self always may be, once we abandon the idea of a unitary subject. And one important extension of this idea in the scenario is that the writer is his own reader.

Now James's critical essays attempt to draw the reader into their bounded economy. 'In every novel the work is divided between the writer and the reader; but the writer makes the reader, very much as he makes his characters.'[57] And the well-made reader is the active reader. James was notably 'modern' in this respect, and carried the idea very far in his personal practice. This was the hazard of sending him a manuscript; you would receive a charming letter explaining that James, perverse monster that he was, could simply not read except by way of 'reconstruction' or 'rehandling'; and so the demolition would follow. Some such drive went into the revisions of the New York Edition; and the scenario mode is specifically designed to provoke it. I might add the obvious point that in the literary market-place James's work often received not so much rehandling as rough handling or no handling at all. How gratifying, then, to banish this neglectful other from a world in which 'The teller of a story is primarily . . .

the listener to it, the reader of it too.'[58] Even where (as in the *Autobiography*) there is direct address to a reader, it is notably Olympian and relaxed, quite unlike the precisely specified reader-position in, say, *The Awkward Age*.

The scenario mode also allows subversion of the division between active and passive—as implied in the scenario for 'The Next Time', with its alternation of narrated and narrating first person. But there is one peculiar displacement of agency to note; and this is the appeal, especially in the *Notebooks*, to a figure of inspiration. Some of these appeals, like the invocation to Maupassant noted earlier, are simply gestures towards a formal ideal. Others seem to summon a muse; but the precise locus of its activity, given the disseminated subject, seems unclear. The notorious 'mon bon' is a case in point. This phrase studs the *Notebooks*: 'Trouve donc, mon bon', 'Live with it a little, mon bon', and so on.[59] Just what is being invoked here? Should we translate as, say, 'my good fellow'—which makes it a personal instruction? or as 'my good creative spirit', which might or might not be an aspect of the self? But to polarize this seems forced, when a single passage can exhibit both the pathos that posits a figure and the irony that undermines it; as here, from an entry in 1910:

> the prospect clears and flushes, and my poor blest old Genius pats me so admirably and lovingly on the back that I turn, I screw round, and bend my lips to passionately, in my gratitude, kiss its hand.[60]

In general, then, we can see in the scenario mode a subversion of opposites, particularly so in *A Small Boy and Others*. The ghosts of past impressions, past people, solicit the narrator, swarming round him like the spirits of Hades around Odysseus. At one point he offers a moralized response: 'for whatever it may be worth, I won't pretend to a disrespect for *any* contributive particle.'[61] Yet at another point he can say of a schoolfellow: 'He vanishes, and I dare say I but make him over, as I make everything.'[62] Solicitous impression and active expression are not exclusive alternatives; one can move back and forth through the door that divides them. So it is appropriate that this volume should contain the dream of the Galerie d'Apollon, which can itself be read as an ironic allegory of oppositional structure.

And there is a crucial case of ironized structure at the close. Autobiography is a privileged metonymic form in that it seems to partake of destiny—if only by hindsight. The narrative is going somewhere, and its end is a goal, or at least a significant stage. Now at the end of *A Small Boy*, the protagonist is ill in bed, and gets up to try to ring the bell. Here are the final lines:

> The question of whether I really reached and rang it was to remain lost afterwards in the strong sick whirl of everything about me, under which I fell into a lapse of consciousness that I shall conveniently here treat as a considerable gap.[63]

In the first place, this is a comic confusion of levels; the activity of the narrated subject is allowed to stand in for that of the narrating subject, who cannot even bother to finish his book himself. And the dignity of autobiography is slighted; the goal turns out to be a gap, and destiny is replaced by accident. Here, as elsewhere in James, the end figures as cessation rather than closure. But closure—with the full formal definition and exclusion that it implies—would be inappropriate. The gate of Janus was closed only in the rare event of universal peace; and, for James as for Stevens, writing is 'a war that never ends'.[64]

## NOTES

1. Morris Shapira (ed.), *Henry James: Selected Literary Criticism* (Harmondsworth: Penguin Books, 1963), p. 218. (Hereafter 'Shapira'.)
2. F. O. Matthiessen and Kenneth Murdock (eds.), *The Notebooks of Henry James* (New York: Oxford University Press, 1961), pp. 89, 100. (Hereafter *Notebooks*.)
3. The material in this paragraph is taken from N. G. L. Hammond and H. H. Scullard (eds.), *The Oxford Classical Dictionary*, Second Edition (Oxford: Clarendon Press, 1970), p. 561, and Catherine B. Avery (ed.), *The New Century Classical Handbook* (London: Harrap, 1962), p. 611.
4. Cf. Richard Palmer, 'Postmodernity and Hermeneutics', *boundary 2*, V.2, Winter 1977, 385.
5. Cf. J. Laplanche and J.-B. Pontalis, *The Language of Psycho-Analysis* (London: The Hogarth Press, 1980), pp. 127–30.
6. R. P. Blackmur, introduction, *The Art of the Novel: Critical Prefaces by Henry James* (New York: Charles Scribner's Sons, 1962), p. 84. (Hereafter 'Prefaces'.)

7. Cf. Jacques Derrida, 'La Loi du genre/The Law of Genre', *Glyph 7* (Baltimore: Johns Hopkins University Press, 1980), pp. 176–229.
8. *The Golden Bowl*, Part Second, Ch. viii (Penguin edn.), p. 125; F. W. Dupee (ed.), *Henry James: Autobiography* (London: W. H. Allen, 1956), p. 198. (Hereafter *Autobiography*.)
9. Shapira, p. 92.
10. *Autobiography*, pp. 442, 274.
11. Shapira, p. 86; *Autobiography*, pp. 60, 254.
12. James E. Miller (ed.), *Theory of Fiction: Henry James* (Lincoln: University of Nebraska Press, 1972), p. 139. (Hereafter 'Miller'.)
13. *Autobiography*, p. 98.
14. *Autobiography*, p. 253.
15. Miller, p. 96.
16. Cf. Charles Rosen and Henri Zerner, 'What Is, and Is Not, Realism?', *New York Review of Books*, XXIX 2, 18 February 1982, 26.
17. Cf. Meyer Shapiro, *Modern Art; 19th and 20th Centuries* (London: Chatto & Windus, 1978), pp. 190–91.
18. Leon Edel, *Henry James: The Conquest of London, 1870–1873* (London: Rupert Hart-Davis, 1962), p. 241.
19. Edel, op. cit., p. 335.
20. Jacques Derrida, *Positions* (London: Athlone Press, 1981), p. 32.
21. John Pilling, *Autobiography and Imagination: Studies in Self-Scrutiny* (London, Boston and Henley: Routledge and Kegan Paul, 1981), p. 28.
22. *Autobiography*, pp. 191–97, contains all material for this paragraph.
23. Sigmund Freud, *The Interpretation of Dreams* (Harmondsworth: Penguin Books, 1980), pp. 427–31. Peter Brooks, *The Melodramatic Imagination* (New Haven: Yale University Press, 1976).
24. Wallace Stevens, *The Necessary Angel: Essays on Reality and the Imagination* (London: Faber and Faber, 1960), p. 36.
25. Cf. Walter Benn Michaels, 'Writers Reading: James and Eliot', *M.L.N.*, 91, 5 October 1976, 837, on the problem of agency as disreputable.
26. *Autobiography*, p. 42. This material is discusssed in an excellent article by Millicent Bell, ' "Art Makes Life": James's Autobiography' in *Revue Francaise d'Etudes Américaines*, 14 May 1982, p. 216. Professor Bell also preceded me in questioning the impressionist subject.
27. Cf. Rainer Nägele in *New German Critique*, No. 16, Winter 1979, 8.
28. Miller, p. 122.
29. Prefaces, pp. 65–6.
30. Miller, p. 82.
31. *Notebooks*, p. 347.
32. F. O. Matthiessen (ed.), *The James Family* (New York: Alfred A. Knopf, 1961), p. 611.
33. Theodora Bosanquet, *Henry James at Work* (London: The Hogarth Press, 1924), p. 32.
34. Prefaces, p. 258.
35. Leon Edel, *Henry James: The Untried Years, 1843–1870* (London: Rupert Hart-Davis, 1953), p. 67.
36. Prefaces, p. 36.

37. Shapira, pp. 376–77.
38. Henry James, *Theatricals: Two Comedies* (London: Osgood, McIlvanie & Co., 1894), p. vi.
39. Henry James, *Theatricals: Second Series* (London: Osgood, McIlvanie & Co., 1895), pp. vi, x.
40. Op. cit., p. xiv.
41. Loc. cit.
42. *Autobiography*, p. 123.
43. *Autobiography*, p. 150.
44. Jacques Derrida, *Spurs/Eperons* (Chicago and London: University of Chicago Press, 1978), pp. 110–11.
45. A point not made in Stephen Donadio, *Nietzsche, Henry James, and the Artistic Will* (New York: Oxford University Press, 1978).
46. Prefaces, p. 52.
47. Marc Shell, *The Economy of Literature* (Baltimore and London: Johns Hopkins University Press, 1978), p. 89. The Longinus reference is on p. 103.
48. Prefaces, p. 84.
49. Prefaces, p. 45.
50. Jonathan Culler, *The Pursuit of Signs: Semiotics, Literature, Deconstruction* (London and Henley: Routledge and Kegan Paul, 1981), pp. 158–59; for further references see pp. 234–35.
51. *Notebooks*, p. 320.
52. *Autobiography*, p. 495.
53. Leon Edel and Gordon N. Ray (eds.), *Henry James & H. G. Wells* (London: Rupert Hart-Davis, 1959), p. 128; Prefaces, p. 321.
54. Cf. Laplanche and Pontalis, op. cit., p. 259.
55. *Notebooks*, pp. 201–3.
56. *Notebooks*, p. 364.
57. Miller, p. 321.
58. Prefaces, p. 63.
59. *Notebooks*, pp. 148, 153.
60. *Notebooks*, p. 357.
61. *Autobiography*, p. 65.
62. *Autobiography*, p. 227.
63. *Autobiography*, p. 236.
64. *The Collected Poems of Wallace Stevens* (London: Faber and Faber, 1955), p. 407.

# 8

# Some Slight Shifts in the Manner of the Novel of Manners

by RICHARD GODDEN

1

The foundation of manners is economic, and as economic structures change so manners change. But what does it mean to argue for an economy of manners? An elaborate place setting, involving careful discrimination as to the position of the fish knives, bears witness to an accumulation of knowledge made manifest. That knowledge depends upon leisure time, which in turn derives from a secure property base. As Veblen put it in 1899, 'the pervading principle and abiding test of good breeding is the requirement of a substantial and patent waste of time.'[1] *The Theory of the Leisure Class* introduces the phrases, 'conspicuous leisure' and 'conspicuous consumption', as it makes the case that leisure is not indolence but a state of high competition, in which the weaponry may range from a classical education to pedigree dogs, but where the prize is constant—the prize being the right to social 'emulation'. When Mr. Sillerton Jackson notes that the Archers' butler has not been told, 'never to slice cucumbers with a steel knife',[2] the reader of *The Age of Innocence* is aware that marginal repositioning has occurred among the first hundred families of New York. For Veblen that gentleman's saliva would be a highly wrought artefact, an 'immaterial' object offering 'serviceable evidence of an unproductive expenditure of time' (p. 47). Such items protest both their naturalness and their intrinsicality, even as they enact a symbolic pantomime of mastery—'If you lack the etiquette don't sit at the tables.' Each makes plain in its 'quasi' artistic, 'quasi' honorific (p. 47) status, its distance from the market place upon which its very development depends; as Veblen puts it, 'the leisure class live by the industrial community rather than in it' (p. 164).

A silver palate and a keen grip on the fish knives are as valued by the late nineteenth-century leisure class as are the Kula objects that circulate among high-ranking male Trobriand islanders:

> the most precious are the oldest, which have been transferred the most carefully and hardly ever displayed. Their names are known, and it is an honour to have one's own name associated with the name of a famous valuable. Indeed what is being transacted in the top sphere is really shared knowledge about a network of mutual confidence. The actual goods are the visible tip of the iceberg. The rest is a submerged classified catalogue of names of persons, places, objects, and dates. The main activity is a continuous attempt to standardize their values as precisely as possible.[3]

The meaning, indeed the very materiality, of such objects is separate from utility or function; it consists in their capacity to bear names and to carry distinctions. Leisure-class objects are good to think rather than to use, for in thinking them those in the know take confidence as to their hold on an information network that adds up to cultural power. The prestige attendant upon an object intensifies in exact proportion to the number of discriminations sedimented within it. For example, Veblen's leisure class expends great energy breeding pedigree dogs, while the van der Lydens, first among Wharton's New York families, tend orchids; the acme of each form is an exemplar that perishes almost as it is conceived: the perfect pug has a face so flat that an operation is required at birth to free its nasal passages, the finest orchid is but a brief flower. Rarefication attends privileged surfaces from the Trobriand Islands to the novels of James; whether or not Gilbert Osmond (*The Portrait of a Lady*) or Adam Verver (*The Golden Bowl*) stand

ethically judged, their tendency to turn person and thing into
'a rarity, an object of beauty, an object of price . . . a *morceau de
musée*'⁴ typifies a habit of perception wider than their own. In
the Preface to *Spoils* James observes:

> Life being all inclusion and confusion, and art being all
> discrimination and selection, the latter, in search of the hard
> latent *value* with which alone it is concerned, sniffs around the
> mass as instinctively and unerringly as a dog suspicious of some
> buried bone. The difference here, however, is that while the dog
> desires his bone but to destroy it, the artist finds in *his* tiny
> nugget, washed free of awkward accretions and hammered into
> a sacred hardness, the very stuff for a clear affirmation, the
> happiest chance for the indestructible.⁵

For James 'surfaces' are less elements in an historical context
than they are crystallizations of aesthetic information. The
most casual object or perspective inclines, via the labour of
informed perception, toward a collector's item. Indeed, a
capacity for 'discrimination and selection' seems, in *The
Bostonians*, to condition physique. Those who possess the social
graces, most manifestly Mrs. Farrinder and Mrs. Burrage, are
given to 'angularity',⁶ while poverty of manner results in poor
shape. To exist in 'the social dusk of that mysterious
democracy' (p. 79) is to suffer a 'vagueness of boundary'
(p. 37); Miss Birdseye is pursued by synonyms for 'formless'
(p. 38), among which 'muffled in laxity' (p. 51) is mighty, and
Mr. Tarrant transcends the 'weary-looking overcoats' (p. 40)
of his peers, in a waterproof that rarely leaves his person and
totally obscures it. Where social discretion aids muscular tone
(it is to be remembered that Madam Merle, that most socially
equipped female, is 'too complete'⁷), mental tone is necessarily
structured around a recognition of distinctions. Jamesian
'appreciation' is quite literally mannered, in that, like items
gracing a bourgeois drawing-room, his observations never
exhaust themselves in the function they serve—be that
denotation or advancing action—rather they take on the
significance of prestige. They no longer designate 'the world',
but the being and social acumen of the observer—they are
accumulative.⁸ At the risk of straining the analogy between
perceptual habit and drawing-room, both are solid with and

through cumulative nicety, where the term 'solid' applies equally to observation, furnishing and business enterprise.

'Interior' too, for the 'solid' Victorian, was a term involving the person and her room. For Hobsbawm 'the home' is 'the quintessential bourgeois world',[9] in which objects may modify owners. Furnishings,

> had value in themselves as expressions of personality, as both the programme and the reality of bourgeois life, even as transformers of man. In the home all these were expressed and concentrated. Hence its internal accumulation.[10]

The pressure of furniture on selfhood is well caught by Wharton in a description of an 1870s interior:

> There was something about the luxury of the Welland house and the density of the Welland atmosphere, so charged with minute observances and exactions, that always stole into his system like a narcotic. The heavy carpets, the watchful servants, the perpetually reminding tick of disciplined clocks, the perpetually renewed stack of cards and invitations on the hall table, the whole chain of tyrannical trifles binding one hour to the next, and each member of the household to all the others, made any less systematized and affluent existence seem unreal and precarious.[11]

Time and the air are created by the latent law of manners made plain through decoration. Time is retrospective where a clock 'remind(s)' the present that the past is its measure and corrective. Each social season in Wharton's New York repeats the events of the previous season. Received manners give form and protect that form from change. Not surprisingly, the carpet is 'heavy', the atmosphere 'narcotic' and the stack of cards, though it changes, remains the same. Taste, in the 1870s, must encourage inertia in order to proclaim the stability of the accumulated wealth from which it arises. Not all the decade's 'interiors' are simply 'solid'; Olive Chancellor's 'parlor', viewed by her Southern cousin, manages to ally habitual taste with curiosity:

> it seemed to him he had never seen an interior that was so much an interior as this queer corridor-shaped drawing-room of his new-found kinswoman; he had never felt himself in the presence of so much organized privacy or of so many objects

159

that spoke of habits and tastes. . . . he had never before seen so many accessories. The general character of the place struck him as Bostonian: this was, in fact, very much what he had supposed Boston to be. He had always heard Boston was a city of culture, and now there was culture in Miss Chancellor's tables and sofas, in the books that were everywhere, on little shelves like brackets (as if a book were a statuette), in the photographs and water-colours that covered the walls, in the curtains that were festooned rather stiffly in the doorways. (p. 27)

Everything is protected and surrounded: the doors by the curtains, the books by the shelves, while the word 'interior' encloses itself. At one level, the framing serves purposes of display, however its very redundancy teeters on the edge of sequestration. A drawing room that is 'corridor-shaped' begs a question as to where it leads—inwards or outwards? The reader might risk an answer, in that he already knows that the proprietor suffers 'fits' of shyness, during which she is 'unable to meet even her own eyes in the mirror' (p. 22). Olive's elusive self-image is the key to her room's instability: 'the Chancellors belonged to the *bourgeoisie*—the oldest and best' (p. 42). One of their daughters, Mrs. Luna, fulfils the 'conspicuous' duties of her leisure, the other longs 'to put off invidious differences and mingle in the common life' (p. 33). Since 'invidious difference' is a structural principle of bourgeois accessories, Olive is at odds with her own room. The Welland's 'home' is a seamless network of information. Olive's objects 'speak' 'culture' item by item, each frame ennobles its object and so, as an ensemble, the room is a show. James's hint of the catalogue implies more than the perceiver's Southern-ness; a little 'stiff', it catches the uncertainty of Olive's 'queer' social trajectory.

Whatever the distinction drawn between these rooms as economic messages, they would both have been read by their contemporaries as feminized spaces. By the mid-nineteenth century, increasing industrial production consolidated a clear distinction between 'home' and 'market', 'leisure' and 'labour'. The latter, in each case, was a male sphere associated with competition, aggression and self-seeking. Deprived of her earlier rôle as a producer within the domestic economy, the mid-nineteenth century woman learned to consume. What

160

man earned, at least in the middle class, woman displayed. The 'home' became a 'separate sphere' in which 'nurture', 'sensibility', 'influence' and 'consumption' might be practised as compensatory labour, at once legitimating economic dependency, while granting a limited identity.[12] Veblen is skeptical as to whether this alternative rôle extends far beyond display among the leisured. He notes that the woman is a 'badge', 'prize' and 'trophy', and that any degree of exemption from labour marks only her husband's accumulations—insofar as 'she is useless and expensive . . . she is consequently valuable evidence of pecuniary strength' (p. 107). As with pugs, so with wives, rarefication in search of inutility and distinction has physical consequences:

> The corset is, in economic theory, substantially a mutilation, undergone for the purpose of lowering the subject's vitality and rendering her permanently and obviously unfit for work . . . but the loss suffered on that score is offset by the gain in reputability which comes of her visibly increased expensiveness and infirmity. (p. 121)

One does not have to agree with Veblen on corsets to recognize that, in a culture where labour and property are the means to 'authoritative selfhood',[13] a woman's individuality is threatened by the demise of domestic industry,[14] and is only marginally redeemed by 'motherhood' and 'marble palaces' (the department stores that proliferated during the 1870s).

In her double rôle as display case and womb, or womb-to-be, the bourgeois woman had also to constitute herself as the antithesis of the male; her passivity must soften his activity, his aggression should elicit her sensitivity so that female unselfishness might modify his necessary selfishness. Deformity, invisibility and amnesia stalk such a selfhood. The woman, at the centre of her drawing-room, becomes the medium through which the man forgets labour and transforms consumption into sentimental privacy and into art.[15] Consequently, the novel of manners is preoccupied with the transfer of such cultural *shamen*: that is to say, with marriage as a dicey exchange of accumulations in their double form as economic fact and cultural artefact (or veil). Consider Wharton's description of the young and recently married May Welland:

161

Perhaps that faculty of unawareness was what gave her eyes their transparency and her face the look of representing a type rather than a person; as if she might have been chosen to pose for a Civic Virtue or a Greek goddess. The blood that ran so close to her fair skin might have been a preserving fluid rather than a ravaging element; yet her look of indestructible youthfulness made her seem neither hard nor dull, but only primitive and pure. (p. 167)

The woman, viewed by her husband, becomes statuesque—her blood, through which his property will be transferred, is 'preserving fluid', and her eye, at least to his eye, is 'transparent', there is nothing behind it to resist his purposes, she is pure to the point of becoming a tabula rasa upon which he may write. Such properties belong, not to one character, but to a 'type' that elicits male desire among the leisured. 'Artefact', 'Innocence', 'Preservative', are standard features that can be variously permed. Verena Tarrant is to Ransom a 'moving statue' (p. 62) and a 'picture' (p. 63), while Mr. Burrage, 'liked her for the same reason that he liked old enamels and old embroideries' (p. 136). The 'brightness of her nature' (p. 61) strains the lexicon of virginity; the more Verena 'shines', the more she inclines to that ultimate male bolt-hole—the white page on which may be written a sentimental novel and a balance sheet. Even her voice, her singular contribution to feminism, is 'pure and rich' (p. 230), a fashion to be 'tasted' (p. 234), found 'sweet' (p. 65), and consumed. Since James gives us little of what she says, and much of how she says it, it is to be presumed that he trusts Ransom's ear. Pansy Osmond is simply the essence of the model; her stepmother learns that to be a lady is to be a portrait, and consents to the frame in part to protect a ward, 'so formed and finished' as to be 'a sheet of blank paper'.[16] *The Portrait of a Lady* was published in 1881, but as late as 1925 leisure-class functions continue to disembody the leisured females of fiction. Daisy Buchanan, named for the flower of innocence, first appears in *The Great Gatsby* in 'white', 'ballooned' seemingly weightless among billowing curtains. Formed to display, she has repressed her body and cashed in her voice, which is described as 'full of money'.[17] In contradistinction, the body of the working-class woman, Myrtle Wilson, uncommitted to the production of manners, is described most frequently in terms of 'blood', 'flesh' and 'vitality'.

From May Welland to Daisy Buchanan, the wealthy female in her feminized space (that most immaterial of 'immaterial objects') protects and distributes the accumulations of her class. She is the guardian of what Lionel Trilling calls 'culture's hum and buzz of implication':

> What I understand by manners . . . is culture's hum and buzz of implication. I mean the whole evanescent context in which its explicit statements are made. It is that part of a culture which is made up of half-uttered or unuttered or unutterable expressions of value. They are hinted at by small actions, sometimes by the arts of dress or decoration, sometimes by tone, gesture, emphasis or rhythm, sometimes by the words that are used with a special frequency or a special meaning. They are the things that for good or bad draw the people of a culture together and that separate them from the people of another culture. They make the part of a culture which is not art, or religion, or morals, or politics, and yet it relates to all these highly formulated departments of culture. It is modified by them; it modifies them; it is generated by them; it generates them. In this part of culture assumption rules, which is often stronger than reason.[18]

Trilling's claims are questionable in that they suppress conflicts of class and gender. The degree to which the notion of 'culture' as an 'evanescent' and 'unuttered' 'context' obscures the presence of uttered contradictions is exactly the measure of the definition's usefulness as an account of what the well-mannered thought manners to be towards the close of the nineteenth century. To speak the fact that the cards that mount on the Welland's hall table are an act of class control—whereby the bourgeoisie monitor the meetings of their sons and daughters who, with the development of the department store and the park, were mingling in new ways[19]—is to insist that as economic patterns shift so manners shift. Frederick Olmsted designed parks explicitly to offer, to the rising proletariat, a horticultural version of the 'softening and refining' 'tea table' of the middle class.[20] The 'marble palaces' were built to guarantee the viability of that tea table; as temples to advertising they sought sufficient sales to cover the

drastically increased production that resulted from the consolidated investment of the '80s and '90s. To read Central
Park or a corset as economic facts is to blow Trilling's cover
and to submit manners to the shifting history of capital and its
accumulations.

## 2

If that history is, from 1850–1900, largely a story of
expansion and accumulation of resource, it is clear that during
the opening two decades of the new century the very form of
capital was seen to change—and with it the form of manners.
But first some facts and figures. While a worker's income
increased by an average of 11% between 1923 and 1929,
corporate profit rose in the same period by 62% and corporate
dividends by 65%. The reason for this may be glossed in two
terms, 'centralization' and 'standardization'. Mergers were
endemic; from 1919 to 1930, 8,000 businesses disappeared.
Among the most significant fields of takeover were electricity
and banking; the electric generator, primary machine of
what has been called the second industrial revolution, was
incorporated.[21] Even as the energy that drove industrial
capital centralized, so the credit that financed expansion
passed into fewer and fewer hands; large banks swallowed
small banks or established branches that took their business,
so that by 1929 1% of the banking facilities of the country
controlled over 46% of the nation's banking resources.[22] Well
financed, mergers fell into two waves reaching peaks between
1897 and 1905 and during the second half of the '20s. Their
form was also twofold: the horizontal merger involved the
absorption of a number of competitors in a given field by one
producer; the vertical merger (more popular in the '20s) saw
one corporation buy out its suppliers or its customers. Both
forms relieved the capitalist of his fear of the glutted market
since the new corporation could limit competition by setting
price and production levels. The net effect of centralization
was an increasing rationalization of resources, and with it
fresh fears of an excess capacity. To ensure continuous and full
use of their accumulations, firms had to move into new
markets and to develop new lines. Each expansion put greater

strain on the running of production, and a managerial revolution coupled with the multiplication of national distribution systems simply fuelled the cause of standardized and efficient administration.

By the '20s 'administration' was gargantuan in ambition; as scientific management and technological innovation guaranteed that expanding and incorporating capital could produce cheaply, advertising sought to monitor and create market needs:

> Advertising has to deal with the greatest principles underlying the relation of man to man. . . . It is the medium of communication between the world's greatest forces—demand and supply. It is a more powerful element in human progress than steam or electricity. . . . That this state of things [the neglect of advertising] will continue, cannot be possible, and men may look forward to a day when advertising will be what it has long deserved to be, one of the world's great sciences. (1893)[23]

The copywriter failed to note that his copy would become 'an aggressive device of corporate survival'.[24] By 1920 it was plain that only by controlling desire could corporate capital reproduce itself. The 'captain of industry' had to become the 'captain of consciousness' if his accumulations were to survive; not surprisingly, between 1900 and 1930 national advertising revenues increased thirteenfold.

Statistics can indicate the quantity of change but miss the qualitative shift. What one witnesses between 1900 and 1930 is a shift in economic emphasis from 'accumulation' to 'reproduction'. A monopoly is inherently less responsive to market fluctuation than other systems of manufacture; its profitability is geared to a large number of invariable overheads that have to be maintained through slump or boom. The corporation can lay off men or reduce wages; it cannot so easily forgo interest payments on loans or insurance, nor can it cease to maintain its research programmes, its plant or rent. Therefore, in order to preserve its own huge accumulation, it must look to the future (and to the distant future), that is, to the problem of 'reproduction'. Put crudely—by 1900 the accumulated capital exists; the real issue is how to produce sufficient profit to support that accumulation. Neither Taylor's time-and-motion studies, nor Ford's flow production, in and of themselves, offer adequate protection, because high productivity can yield the necessary profit only if the markets are primed to consume what has been produced.

Arguably, the consumer is the most important product of late capitalism; he is the primary machine without which 'the very play time of the people' could not be 'run . . . into certain moulds'[25]:

> Consumption is the name given to the new doctrine; and it is admitted today to be the greatest idea that America has given to the world; the idea that the workmen and masses be looked upon not simply as workers and producers, but as *consumers*. . . . Pay them more, sell them more, prosper more is the equation.[26]

In the words of Paula Fass, analysing collegiate youth in the '20s, 'the big sell had become synonymous with America's contribution to Western Civilization.'[27] High schools and colleges prepared students for corporate employment via peer group instruction in conformity and competition; their graduates were the new intellectual proletariat who would service the managerial revolution, while consuming the high output to which that revolution contributed:

> Competition within conformity and conformity in the service of competition were the structuring facts of campus life in the twenties . . . values that in a specific American social context were made to read like a twentieth century text on business success and consumer habits.[28]

Note—'consumer habits'; the employee as worker *and* consumer contributes to the reproduction of surplus value—accumulation is frowned upon while indulgence is blessed. At both domestic and national levels the American economy was running on high credit in that the institution of credit allows speedier production and speedier consumption. Consequently, 'to be wholly part of the economic life of the new society, the young had to be *not* accumulating entrepreneurs but at once workers and consumers.'[29]

All this may seem a disturbing distance from fish knives and the true taste of cucumber; the gap marks a considerable transition in manners. Though the Jamesian interior may well manifest conspicuous leisure and conspicuous consumption, it cannot guarantee a high turnover in consumption, and it positively mitigates against a truly mass market for the items that it contains. Those items are 'solid', even as the manners that surround them are 'solid' (so scrupulously learned as to appear innate). What capital increasingly needs after 1900 is a highly mobile, highly reproducible and highly controllable system of manners. That is to say, fashion must supplant manners; where taste once stood, style must stand. Manners and taste are cumulative and integrative; indeed the selfhood that they realize is its own ultimate possession. Fashions and styles are equally an extension of capital, but of capital focused on the sphere of reproduction. Fashion penetrates the mannered self and opens it for the market. The new 'science' of advertising invested heavily in social insecurity. The consumer of the '20s was taught to denigrate his own body; 'paralysed pores', 'vacation knees', 'ashtray breath' and 'spoon fed face' may be dated diseases, but the sustained economic assault on the consumer's 'integrity' is far from over, and its direction is ever inwards—witness vaginal deodorants and suppository selling. The problem lies in the finances of the corporate body, and not in the sweetness of the bodies on the street. Likewise, the solution is corporate; the consumer, anxious and amnesiac, must forget his deficient 'self', and purchase the selves made available to him by the business community. A current example may catch the experience more fully—it is a commonplace that we associate particular times in our lives with popular songs, more particularly with the melody line of a record. Consequently, when we hear the old song we *feel* old; the market, in order to instigate a profitable turnover of styles, foreshortens the feeling of ageing. Therefore, we who have bought a musical style and identified ourselves through it, experience a death (albeit of a manufactured phase of life) even as the style changes. The experience contains a particular kind of self-knowledge; we who bought feel sold out, and therefore recognize the workings of the market within us. Various reactions are possible—a contempt for the old style (now a part of ourselves), rage at the market switch (which is in us and is self-loathing), or purchase of the old style, when eventually and inevitably it is made new and repriced by nostalgia (which is to buy back our own memory).[30] Fashion is always *dis*integrative; it aims to give us several selves, thereby providing capital with a diversification of markets.

One way of focusing the interconnected histories of self and of capital is to present their liaison in schematic form:

| *Sphere of Accumulation* | *Sphere of Reproduction* |
|---|---|
| Inertia of Capital ('emulation') | High turnover of capital (mass market) |
| Leisure Class | Culture Industry |
| Manners | Fashion |
| Integrative selfhood (A drawing-room) | Disintegrative selfhood (Hollywood) |

Or as Mandel puts it, almost as schematically:

> The real consequences of the reduced turnover-time of fixed capital . . . is a shift in the emphasis of the activity of the major owners of capital. In the age of freely competitive capitalism, this emphasis lay principally in the immediate sphere of production, and in the age of classical imperialism in the sphere of accumulation (the dominance of financial capital); today, in the age of late capitalism, it lies in the sphere of reproduction.[31]

Fitzgerald's writing straddles the transition from 'classical imperialism' to 'late capitalism', and is an extremely sensitive register of it. Daisy Buchanan is a display case for leisure-class wealth, yet she is drawn to Gatsby. Where Tom Buchanan's money is inherited and his body solid ('cruel', 'capable of leaverage'[32]), Gatsby's assets are quite literally liquid—he heads a bootlegging empire, and his voice sounds like a quick flick 'through a dozen magazines'.[33] Daisy assures him, ' "You resemble the advertisement of the man," she went on innocently, "You know, the advertisement of the man—" '[34] her sentence remains unfinished because Gatsby embodies every conceivable selling line. His selfhood, at least to Daisy's eye, is as liquid as his assets. The structure of Daisy's desire is economic, her adultery is hot for the new activities of the new owners of the new capital, and therefore its location shifts from the drawing-room of East Egg to Gatsby's lawns, where parties epitomize mobility, and 'romance' enters the sphere of reproduction:

Almost the last thing I remember was standing with Daisy
and watching the moving-picture director and his Star. They
were still under the white-plum tree and their faces were
touching except for a pale, thin ray of moonlight between. It
occurred to me that he had been very slowly bending toward
her all evening to attain this proximity, and even while I
watched I saw him stoop one ultimate degree and kiss at her
cheek.

'I like her,' said Daisy, 'I think she's lovely.'

But the rest offended her—and inarguably, because it wasn't
a gesture but an emotion.[35]

'Emotion' and 'gesture' are carefully distinguished; 'emotion'
implies an integral self that feels, 'gesture' locates that self
outside in a repeatable event. As the director kisses his star, he
constructs a movie still that might be used to advertise a film
or to promote a style. Daisy is excited because she can see
herself, and consume herself, in the mirror of that highly
marketable gesture.

The two novels that follow *The Great Gatsby* chart Fitzgerald's
sense of the changing structures of capital. *Tender is the Night*
(1939) centres on the career of a psychiatrist, Dick Diver, who
treats and eventually marries the incestuously spoiled
daughter of the Warrens, a noted Chicago family. Incest could
be read as an economic crime; the father, rather than
exchange his daughter, penetrates her as he might penetrate a
market, and accumulates her sexuality to his own. Incest is
integrative in its denial of the mixing of different bloods and
classes. Dick's marriage, therefore, ties him to an absolute
'token' of the leisure class. However, Nicole cannot be
exchanged fully since, at a subconscious level, she has been
locked up among her father's assets. Dick's attention duly
wanders to Rosemary Hoyt, a film star whose first success was
*Daddy's Girl*. Rosemary, too, is the child of capital, but her
image belongs to the culture industry and so is liable to
endless reproduction. In taking Rosemary, Dick escapes from
the sphere of accumulation—in whose traumatic bed he must
replay the acquisitiveness of the greedy father—only to enter
the sphere of reproduction, where, although he turns down a
screen test, he comes apart, sensing in his every move a
gesture without substance.

169

Fitzgerald's final novel, *The Last Tycoon* (1941), does not veer between economic spheres; it is almost hermetically set in a Hollywood studio, where its hero is a producer responsible for the reproduction of reality in a consumable form. When Munroe Stahr falls in love, he does so with a woman who reminds him of the screen image of his dead wife—an image that he helped to conceive. Stahr is the perfect capitalist; if all men were Stahr the fixed overheads on corporate investment would constitute no risk to profitability, since there could be no overproduction or under-consumption. Stahr consumes what he produces, and his products (Minna Davis, his first wife) standardize and predicate his needs (Kathleen, his mistress).

### 3

If the framework that I have outlined may be used to map shifts within one literary career, it ought to facilitate close readings of particular novels. *The Bostonians* (1886) is a useful example because it deals with the relationship between advertising and manners, and does so at a problematic moment within the history of capital. Despite its publication date it would be wrong to fix *The Bostonians* in what Mandel calls 'the sphere of accumulation', in part because of the difficulty of specifying dates for economic phases—for example, there is the suggestion that by the 1840s Lowell's textile production was 'a miniature of the corporate industrial society of the twentieth century'.[36] The real problem is to decide when a system of economic organization is sufficiently widespread to produce social patterns that may be said to be typical.

By the 1870s, the decade in which the novel is set, the post Civil War boom had glutted the market, inducing slump and necessitating forced 'combinations' to control price and production. In 1882 the Standard Oil Company formed the first trust, and by 1889 New Jersey, sensing the drift to 'consolidation',[37] amended her incorporation law to allow one trust to purchase the stocks of another. Provision for the general incorporation of holding companies was rapidly instigated by other states. Verena and Ransom court in a ruined shipyard; Ransom's business in New York is sparse. The 1870s were, indeed, a decade of depression; however, by 1886 the first great corporate enterprises had appeared, carrying with them the structural problem of reproduction. 'The need to keep the consolidated production activities working steadily called for close co-ordination with customer demand through the creation of marketing organization.'[38] Boston appears to have been good ground in which to grow advertising agents[39]; Rowell and Dodd opened there in 1865 and, via the *Advertisers Gazette*, pioneered and taught the skills of purchasing newspaper space and retailing to advertisers. The 'new science' was Bostonian in origin, and between 1870 and 1900 it prospered, increasing tenfold in national volume.

Mrs. Luna likens Verena to 'a walking advertisement' (p. 226), and on the day of her great address, 'all the walls and fences of Boston flame[d] . . . with her name' (p. 358). For James, Verena is a spectacle before she is a feminist, and it is with his uncertain response to publicity that I am most concerned. David Howard argues, persuasively, that the novel may be read as an attempt by various persons to gain a managerial influence over Verena.[40] At her début Verena is the medium whereby Selah Tarrant publicizes his own occult powers; from the first this spiritualist was *in* publicity—he started as a door-to-door vendor of lead pencils. Olive Chancellor, quite literally, buys off the father's interest in order to train Verena as an outlet for her ideas on the rights of women (it is envisaged that she will rival Mrs. Farrinder on the lecture circuit). Meanwhile, Verena is variously courted, most symptomatically by Matthias Pardon. James calls Pardon a 'son of his age' because of his 'state of intimacy with the newspapers' and his 'cultivation of the great arts of publicity' (p. 115). Pardon is an early gossip-columnist:

> He regarded the mission of mankind upon earth as a perpetual evolution of telegrams; everything to him was very much the same, he had no sense of proportion or quality; but the newest thing was what came nearest exciting in his mind the sentiment of respect. (p. 116)

Newness excites him because, in a commercial age—an age of 'receding concreteness'—to be new is to appear authentic.

171

The phrase 'receding concreteness' is Adorno's; he argues that, given mass production, the surfaces of the world seem predictable, even as our experience of those surfaces is pre-conditioned:

> The never-changing quality of machine-produced goods, the lattice of socialization that enmeshes and assimilates equally objects and [our] view of them, converts everything encountered into . . . a fortuitous specimen of a species, the *doppel-gänger* of a model. The layer of unpremeditatedness, freedom from intentions . . . seems consumed. Of it the idea of newness dreams. Itself unattainable, newness installs itself . . . amidst the first consciousness of the decay of experience.[41]

Adorno's point is twofold: that hope for the new is an assault on commercial surfaces, and that that hope is false since newness itself is a consumer device. Newness is the shock that sells. For Pardon, Verena is just such a 'sensation' (p. 305). She is an anthology of telegrams to editors—as he tells Mrs. Luna on the eve of the Boston launch:

> We want to know how she feels about tonight; what report she makes of her nerves, her anticipations; how she looks, what she had on, up to six o'clock. . . . But can't you tell me any little personal items—the sort of thing the people like? What is she going to have for supper? or is she going to speak-a-without previous nourishment? (p. 362)

Adorno consigns the recession of concreteness to 'decay'; it should be remembered, however, that sensation and the sensory object also have a history. 'Decay' is historically imprecise. For Veblen the materials of the leisure class are *made*; their structure may be a network of false distinctions, but their manufacture takes time. Consequently, Olive Chancellor's 'interior' is a regulative space in which a whole history of leisured labour overtly and silently declares itself. In contradistinction, the kinds of item that appear for sale in newspaper columns and whose brand names are 'inlaid' in the letter-writing tables of hotel vestibules (p. 100) suppress their past. The concreteness of their production must be denied lest it impede the rapidity of their exchange and consumption.[42] Mr. Tarrant is prophetic in his recognition that 'human existence . . . was a huge publicity' (p. 97). He 'haunts' 'editorial elbows' and 'compositors' (p. 100) because he knows that 'newspapers [are] the richest expression . . . of human life'—a sentiment whose validity James was bitterly to confess only in 1903, when he acknowledged that newspapers 'were all the furniture of . . . consciousness'.[43] Furniture matters to James; the confession must have troubled him. Yet Verena is more her father's protégé than she is Olive's; indeed, as a protostar she is entirely at odds with the objects that surround her in the Chancellor drawing-room. They, albeit ambivalently, 'spoke of habits and tastes'; Verena's voice is an assault on all that they might say, since, as organized publicity, Verena is indiscriminately consumable. Her social range is capacious; from the South End of Boston to the salons of New York, from the 'garb of toil' pervaded by 'an odour of India-rubber' (p. 40) to 'the best society' (p. 218), few remain unsold. What she sells matters less than how she sells it. This is her voice to Ransom's ear:

> Her speech, in itself, had about the value of a pretty essay, committed to memory and delivered by a bright girl at an 'academy'; it was vague, thin, rambling, a tissue of generalities that glittered agreeably enough in Mrs. Burrage's veiled lamp-light. . . . He asked himself what either he or any one else would think of it if Miss Chancellor—or even Mrs. Luna—had been on the platform instead of the actual declaimer. Nevertheless, its importance was high, and consisted precisely, in part, of the fact that the voice was not the voice of Olive or of Adeline. Its importance was that Verena was unspeakably attractive, and this was all the greater for him in the light of the fact, which quietly dawned upon him as he stood there, that he was falling in love with her. It had tapped at his heart for recognition, and before he could hesitate or challenge, the door had sprung open and the mansion was illuminated. He gave no outward sign; he stood gazing as at a picture; but the room wavered before his eyes, even Verena's figure danced a little. This did not make the sequel of her discourse more clear to him; her meaning faded again into the agreeably vague, and he simply felt her presence, tasted her voice. (p. 234)

Despite Olive's political concerns, the voice has an oddly similar effect upon her:

> The habit of public speaking, the training, the practice, in which she had been immersed, enabled Verena to unroll a coil

of propositions dedicated even to a private interest with the most touching, most cumulative effect. Olive was completely aware of this, and she stilled herself, while the girl uttered one soft, pleading sentence after another, into the same rapt attention she was in the habit of sending up from the benches of an auditorium. She looked at Verena fixedly, felt that she was stirred to her depths, that she was exquisitely passionate and sincere, that she was a quivering, spotless, consecrated maiden, that she really had renounced [Ransom], that they were both safe. . . . She came to her slowly, took her in her arms and held her long—giving her a silent kiss. From which Verena knew that she believed her. (p. 261)

Verena converts her listeners into an audience and recasts each vocal context as a venue. Her delivery elides the political and the personal to a single promise, singly given—an offer of 'desire' set within a private interior. In a voice, evocative of a 'mansion' behind a door, she displays that icon designed for the bourgeois dream of domestic space, the 'spotless . . . maiden'. Listening, both believe that Verena proposes 'privacy'. To Ransom, 'she was meant . . .—for privacy, for him, for love' (p. 234); to Olive, even the Music Hall must be approached obliquely via a series of secretions. Verena promotes 'love' in a form that has more to do with the mid-century vogue for sentimental fictions than with early feminist advocacy of 'rational love' or 'free unions' (p. 114).[44] Her 'publicity' is all for 'privacy', that is for the 1870s paliative to the increasing coherence of the market; her voice conjures the sentimental within the domestic, and is therefore essential to capital as it gears itself to the dream life of a consumer culture.

As early as 1868, in his *Hints to Advertisers*, David Frohman insists, 'a man can't do business without advertising'[45]; Pardon is of Frohman's persuasion. The columnist appreciates that Verena's manner can absorb any matter—as he insinuates to Olive, she has 'charm' for which there is 'a great demand . . . nowadays in connection with new ideas' (p. 118); 'ideas' in the plural refers to more than the plurality of women's rights. For Pardon, Verena could 'take a new line' (p. 118), presumably on almost anything—she has as many selves as there are available markets. I am reminded of the ubiquity of Orson Welles, or at least of his speech rhythms in television commercials. Welles himself may be under contract to a sherry manufacturer, but his phrasing introduced Victor Borge to Danish lager and is responsible for many a liaison between utterance and commodity. Verena is Welles at a higher pitch. The economics of such voices are 'spectacular', where 'the spectacle is *capital* to such a degree of accumulation that it becomes an image.'[46] Guy Debord's assertion is merely as gnomic as the history that it compresses; to unpack—'degree of accumulation' refers to corporate capital's growing difficulty over the quick realization of surplus value. Only if a product can be promoted can it be sold with seemly haste, therefore its 'image' is of its essence. Labour and price are secondary considerations; like money before it, the capacity to be 'image[d]' (advertised) has become a form of equivalence essential to sociability and so to economic calm.

Though Verena eventually becomes a centre piece in one domestic sphere (the Ransom household), her lexicon of light is for most of the novel capable of double articulation; 'radiant', 'shining', 'brightness', 'living in the gaslight', 'divine spark', 'dazzling' . . . each term or phrase could be read as part of the almost statutory network that submits the woman to the wife and the blank page to the property contract (integrative). However, as Verena perfects 'her brightness . . . her air of being a public character' (p. 198), moving toward 'her real beginning' (p. 305) at the Music Hall, so her illumination inclines to the promotional (disintegrative). James will not face his own split reference because it links the spheres of accumulation and reproduction, a developmental line that ties Verena to Fitzgerald's Rosemary Hoyt and leads eventually to Mailer's Marilyn Monroe. To avoid this economic plot, James marries his problem to a Southern conservative, one of the 'landless' 'landed gentry' (p. 172) who knowingly strikes her 'dumb' (p. 277) and is last seen 'cloak[ing]' and 'conceal[ing]' her face (p. 384), copies of which will subsequently not be worth the paper they are printed on to the select stores of Boston (p. 180).

James appreciates his own dilemma because, as John Goode has argued, 'he is saturated in the values of capitalism; in its metaphysical notions of a substantial self.'[47] Goode's judgement is striking but imprecise; the capital that soaks James is

175

capital in its second phase of 'classical imperialism'; the 'metaphysics of the substantial self' do not belong to late capitalism.
A 'substantial' selfhood is the property of a possessive individual who guarantees his own intrinsicality by possessing
others and resisting his own possession. Olive and Ransom are
nominally of this stamp, yet *The Bostonians*, in terms of its
materials, is awkwardly positioned on the edge of very different
kinds of social relation, and therefore of an alternative selfhood. If 'self' may be said to accord with the pulse of accumulation, as accumulation changes so too does the pulse of the
self. Consequently, Olive's 'pure ego',[48] for all its possessive-
ness, is deeply divided. She is self declaredly of 'the *bourgeoisie*'
(p. 47) and yet, almost literally, tears herself apart. Masochism
is her leitmotif. Since, for Olive, men are 'organized atrocious-
ness' (p. 249), it is only apt that they should also be a 'brutal,
bloodstained ravaging race' capable of all manner of torture
and crucifixion (p. 44). Nonetheless, Olive's suffering crosses
gender lines—she is a Joan of Arc (p. 132) who burns as
readily under Verena's hand as under Ransom's. Indeed,
Ransom and Verena are so allied in Olive's imagination that
they constitute the structure of her masochism. Olive assures
Verena that she had 'a definite prevision' of Verena's first visit
to the Chancellor house; during the same conversation she
explains that such 'forebodings' are 'a peculiarity of her
organization' (p. 77), and offers as further evidence 'the sudden
dread that had come to her . . . after proposing to Mr. Ransom
to go with her to Miss Birdseye's' (p. 78). According to
Verena, her friend's capacity to prophesy depends upon 'force
of will' (p. 78); if so, that will is radically split, projecting
simultaneously a love object and the block to that object.
Ransom is Olive's creation. Her 'intuition' and 'foreboding'
(p. 254) transforms an obscure cousin into a haunting fear
(p. 262), a 'sudden horror' (p. 311) and 'the trap of fate'
(p. 248). His unwanted manifestations strike her as 'fantastic'
(p. 86) to the point of being spectral; he afflicts her as 'dread',
'palpitation' (p. 248) and 'a kind of concussion' (p. 312). It is
important to recognize that her 'wound[s]' (p. 128) are not
only self-inflicted and self-delighting, but are out of all proportion to their cause—unless one considers that impact to be
more than sexual.

René Girard argues that desire cannot come into being without the mediating presence of a third party. By insisting that an Other attends any loving couple he offers access to Olive's tripartite heart:

> Jealousy and envy imply a third presence: object, subject, and a third person toward whom the jealousy or envy is directed. These two 'vices' are therefore triangular; however we never recognize a model in the person who arouses jealousy because we always take the jealous person's attitude toward the problem of jealousy. Like all victims of internal mediation, the jealous person easily convinces *herself* that *her* desire is spontaneous, in other words, that it is deeply rooted in the object and in this object alone. As a result *she* always maintains that *her* desire preceded the intervention of the mediator. *She* would have us see him as an intruder, a bore, a *terzo incomodo* who interrupts a delightful tête-à-tête. Jealousy is thus reduced to the irritation we all experience when one of our desires is accidentally thwarted. But true jealousy is infinitely more profound and complex; it always contains an element of fascination with the insolent rival.[49]

Olive's desire, for all its seeming spontaneity, is mediated by a third who walks always beside her. The simultaneous arrival of intruder and lover indicates the uncertainty of Olive's social position. 'The miseries and mysteries of the People' (p. 104) fascinate but elude her until she discovers feminism, at which point paths to 'the inexpressibly low' (p. 104) seem to open and 'the common life' is more available to 'mingle' with (p. 33). However, the poor come quarantined in oratory; neither 'the social dusk of that mysterious democracy' (p. 79) nor 'the romance of the people' (p. 42) can be stretched to cover the plight of labour in the depression of the '70s:

> The divergence between the interests of employer and worker and the increasing loss of personal contact between the two sides of industry as the scale of manufacturing increased were helping to develop class feeling in the United States; but the great strikes of 1877 acted as a catalyst in making people consciously aware of social distinctions.[50]

'The people', in their negative aspect, are, for Olive, 'Charlie' — a figure in 'a white overcoat and paper collar', a perpetually 'obtrusive swain' ever able to distract 'poor girl[s]' from the ballot (p. 42). If labour is Charlie then labour knows nothing of unions, of the Greenback party, of the 'Molly Maguires' or of twenty-six rioters dead in Pittsburg; such Charlies can be kept out.

The door to Olive's pet project, a hypothetical 'evening club' for female workers, is doubly barred against incursions from the under class. Seen first as poorly paid women and second as a suitor, the real figure already shrouded in 'dusk' is virtually indistinguishable. Ransom is Charlie writ large and different; the disquieting face of the proletarian is replaced by the troubling smile of the dispossessed gentry. Recast as a proprietor without property, who, despite defeat, embodies national unity (does he not visit a war memorial to his enemy?), Charlie vanishes under his masks. And yet no displacement entirely forgets its path; the archaeology of Ransom's quasi-spectral effect goes some way to explain his energies in Olive's mind. Olive needs Ransom as much as she needs Verena. His Southernness defers the proletariat, even as his passion recasts a problematic liaison between capital and labour as an essentially bourgeois love-match. The displacements make labour possible for Olive and allow her to approach 'the dusk' (while not seeing it), and, via Verena, to renegotiate a workable relationship with 'the People'.

The Verena affair distances Olive from her class, or at least marks an emphatic shift in how she uses her family monies. As one who previously wished to work among 'pale shop-maidens' (p. 42), her interest in 'the common life' was deeply conservative. The provision of an 'evening club for her fatigued, underpaid sisters' (p. 43), though benefiting the staff of the 'marble palaces', would increase their daytime efficiency and relieve pressure on employers to provide adequate facilities in situ.[51] Such a project, albeit of feminist concern, protects the owners of capital, and more particularly the owners of consumer capital. By working with Verena, Olive does more than protect, she joins those owners. The philanthropist becomes an entrepreneur, handling a new voice. Personal management gives way to business management as Filer is hired to realize Pardon's promotional hint over the suitability of the Music Hall as venue. Olive's commitment to her protégée is both emotional and financial; the extent to which that investment modifies the typical forms of bourgeois accumulation is, however, the measure of her need for the ubiquity of Ransom.

Olive's jealousy is at once formally imaginative and socially repressive; taking shape as 'a sort of mystical foreboding' (p. 240), it contains in miniature a double narrative resolution. Having masked the proletariat, Ransom protects Olive from the unpalatable logic of the development of the bourgeoisie. If Olive is ever to return to 'the oldest and best' drawing-rooms of her class, she must lose Verena to Ransom. The final scene in the antechambers of the Music Hall, with Filer pricing every quarter of a second at $500, and the police at the door to protect the new form of wealth, is not just one of emotional re-alliance. Ransom takes Verena, and in so doing either halts Olive's economic drift or forces her to be a 'spectacle' in her own right. Whether Olive becomes the new 'voice' is a mute point; James shows her 'rush' towards the platform, and notes 'the quick, complete and tremendous silence' (p. 384) which greets her arrival. By maintaining that silence, he effectively deserts Olive at the most interesting point of her career—the moment of 'publicity'—the moment when the self possession of the bourgeoisie must change if it is to ensure both the continuing profitability of its properties and the lasting comforts of a self image that is more than an archaism. However, having granted intrinsic selfhood to Verena, by force of matrimony, it is unlikely that he will disintegrate her manager.

The notion of the disintegral self has no appeal to James; as he wrote to Grace Norton in 1883:

> You are right in your consciousness that we are all echoes and reverberations of the *same*, and you are noble when your interests and pity as to everything that surrounds you, appears to have a sustaining and harmonizing power. Only don't, I beseech you, *generalize* too much as to these sympathies and tendernesses—remember that every life is a special problem which is not yours but another's, and content yourself with the terrible algebra of your own. Don't melt too much into the universe, be as solid and dense as you can.[52]

Verena is a melter, and only the Jamesian commitment to the possessive ego—to the right of everyone to accumulate property in himself (where property provides intrinsicality)—means that she may melt just so far. Late in *The Bostonians* James steps awkwardly back from Verena's approach to the disintegral sphere of reproduction:

> No stranger situation can be imagined than that of these extraordinary young women. . . . it was so singular on Verena's part, in particular, that I despair of presenting it to the reader with the air of reality. To understand it, one must bear in mind her peculiar frankness, natural and acquired, her habit of discussing questions, sentiments, moralities, her education, in the atmosphere of lecture rooms, of *seances*, her familiarity with the vocabulary of emotion, the mysteries of 'the spiritual life.' She had learned to breathe and move in a rarefied air, as she would have learned to speak Chinese if her success in life had depended upon it; but this dazzling trick, and all her artlessly artful facilities, were not part of her essence, an expression of her innermost preferences. What *was* a part of her essence was the extraordinary generosity with which she would expose herself, give herself away, turn herself inside out, for the satisfaction of a person who made demands of her. Olive, as we know, had made the reflection that no one was naturally less preoccupied with the idea of her dignity, and . . . it must be admitted that in reality she was very deficient in the desire to be consistent with herself. (pp. 325–26)

Despite her metamorphic proclivities, and by dint of emphasis rather than argument, Verena retains an 'essence', a structure formed, like the fish knives, from discrimination—'an expression of her innermost *preferences*' (italics mine). Where that property might lodge in a being capable of 'turn[ing] herself inside out' is debatable. Nonetheless, James will have it so. His contradictory defence of the 'solid' and the 'dense' is a form of self-defence, indicating how narrow is his affiliation to one moment of capital and to the uses made of that moment and of that capital by a particular leisure class.

The plot of *The Bostonians*, at the simplest level of who does what to whom (but not for why), is a tissue of displacements. Character relations assume one form rather than another in order to keep out a scarcely seen but ever present threat—labour. Likewise, the aesthetic items most appreciated by James generally crystallize from discriminations which, since they involve the discriminating in comparative judgement and select information, are a form of exclusion. 'Beauty' like plot design keeps Charlie from the door, and so guarantees the security of the contents of the drawing-room. If my analogy is true, *The Bostonians*, in detail and in structure, derives its shape from a singular shift in the history of accumulation.

NOTES

1. Thorstein Veblen, *The Theory of the Leisure Class* (London, 1970), p. 51.
2. Edith Wharton, *The Age of Innocence* (London, 1966), p. 48.
3. Mary Douglas and Baron Isherwood, *The World of Goods* (Harmondsworth, 1978), p. 148.
4. Henry James, *The Golden Bowl*, Vol. 1 (New York, 1909), p. 12.
5. Henry James, *The Art of the Novel* (London, 1948), p. 120.
6. Henry James, *The Bostonians* (London, 1952), p. 38.
7. Henry James, *The Portrait of a Lady* (New York, 1909), p. 361.
8. See Jean Baudrillard, *For a Critique of the Political Economy of the Sign* (St. Louis, 1981), particularly the essay, 'Sign Function and Class Logic', pp. 29–62.
9. Eric Hobsbawm, *The Age of Capital 1848–1875* (New York, 1975), pp. 254–55.
10. Ibid., p. 254.
11. Wharton, *The Age of Innocence*, ed. cit., p. 190.
12. See Ann Douglas, *The Feminization of American Culture* (New York, 1979), particularly Chapter 2, 'Feminine Disestablishment', pp. 44–79; also Elizabeth Fox-Genovese, 'Placing Women's History in History', *New Left Review*, No. 133 (May–June, 1982), 5–29.
13. See Fox-Genovese, loc. cit., 24.
14. Julia Matthaei argues that the emergence of separate sexual spheres worked to the benefit of women: 'The new relationship between man and woman was one of equality and difference, not superior and inferior. Woman, acquiring for the first time a clearly distinct and social sphere, acquired a distinct and different existence from man, and from her husband. . . . Hence woman was no longer considered to be inferior to her male partner, but rather different and equal.' See, *An Economic History of Women in America* (Brighton, 1982), p. 116. I am unpersuaded that 'different' means 'equal', particularly when unsupported by earning power.
15. If such a rôle was palpable fantasy, the work of Anne Douglas and Alfred Habegger reveals how far that fantasy was both real and collective. From the 1840s to the 1880s popular fiction meant fiction for women, by women—a sentimental literature that idealized marriage. As Habegger has it, 'A great deal of nineteenth-century women's fiction was a brew laced with opium, alcohol, a pinch of wormwood and

181

buckets of molasses. It was the moral equivalent of soothing syrup (the male drug being alcohol)' (*Gender, Fantasy and Realism in American Literature* (New York, 1982), p. 31).

16. James, *The Portrait of a Lady*, ed. cit., p. 401.
17. F. Scott Fitzgerald, *The Great Gatsby* (New York, n.d.), p. 120.
18. Lionel Trilling, 'Manners, Morals and the Novel', collected in *The Liberal Imagination* (Harmondsworth, 1970), p. 209.
19. See William Leech, *True Love and Perfect Union: The Feminist Reform of Sex and Society* (London, 1981), p. 239.
20. S. B. Sutton (ed.), *Civilizing American Cities: A Selection of Frederick Law Olmsted's Writings on City Landscapes* (Cambridge, Mass., 1971), pp. 78–9.
21. Between 1902–9 electrical output increased nineteen-fold, while 3,700 utility companies vanished. On mergers more generally see William Leuchtenburg, *The Perils of Prosperity* (Chicago, 1958), pp. 178–203, Douglas Dowd, *The Twisted Dream* (Cambridge, Mass., 1974), pp. 53–77, and Alfred Chandler, Jr., *Strategy and Structure* (Cambridge, Mass., 1962), pp. 1–42 and pp. 383–96.
22. Leuchtenburg, op. cit., p. 192.
23. Copy from a New York agency (1893), quoted in Frank Presbrey, *The History and Development of Advertising* (New York, 1929), p. 341.
24. Stuart Ewen, *Captains of Consciousness: Advertising and the Social Roots of the Consumer* (New York, 1976), p. 54.
25. Robert and Helen Lynd, *Middletown* (New York, 1956), p. 491.
26. Christine Frederick, *Selling Mrs. Consumer* (1929), quoted by Ewen, op. cit., p. 22.
27. Paula Fass, *The Damned and the Beautiful* (Oxford, 1977), p. 257.
28. Ibid., p. 226.
29. Ibid., p. 257.
30. This section of my argument relies heavily on Theodor Adorno's 'Fetish Character in Music and Regression of Listening', collected in *The Essential Frankfurt School Reader*, ed. Andrew Arato and Eike Gebhart (Oxford, 1978), pp. 270–99.
31. Ernest Mandel, *Late Capitalism* (London, 1980), p. 245.
32. Fitzgerald, *The Great Gatsby*, ed. cit., p. 6.
33. Ibid., p. 67.
34. Ibid., p. 119.
35. Ibid., p. 121.
36. Thomas Cochran, quoted by Alan Trachtenberg, *The Incorporation of America: Culture and Society in the Gilded Age* (New York, 1982), p. 7.
37. The distinction between 'combination' and 'consolidation' belongs to Chandler, op. cit., pp. 386–90.
38. Chandler, op. cit., p. 387.
39. See Presbrey, op. cit., p. 266
40. David Howard, 'The Bostonians', collected in *The Air of Reality*, ed. John Goode (London, 1972), pp. 5–35.
41. Theodor Adorno, *Minima Moralia* (London, 1974), p. 235.
42. The drive to eradicate 'production' from 'selling' started early, as *Printers Ink* noted retrospectively in 1938: 'the first advertising told the

name of the product. In the second stage the specifications of the product were outlined. Then came emphasis upon the uses of the product. With each step the advertisers moved further away from the factory viewpoint and edged itself closer into the mental processes of the consumer.' Quoted by Ewen, op. cit., p. 80.

43. Leon Edel (ed.), *The Complete Tales of Henry James*, Vol. XII (Phila-delphia, 1964), p. 14. The judgement is addressed to the popular journalists Maud Blandy and Howard Bight in 'The Papers'; however, its application is plainly more general. See Peter Conn, *The Divided Mind* (Cambridge, 1983), pp. 21–2.

44. For a discussion of this phrase within the context of feminist accounts of 'love' during the latter half of the nineteenth century, see Leech, op. cit., particularly Ch. 5, 'The Vindication of Love', pp. 99–129.

45. Quoted in Anne Douglas, op. cit., p. 66.

46. Guy Debord, *Society of the Spectacle* (Detroit, 1973), section 34.

47. John Goode, 'Character and Henry James', *New Left Review*, No. 40 (Nov./Dec. 1966), 55–75. My argument does scant justice to Goode's subtlety. His preoccupation remains the ways and means by which character for James preserves its identity through strategies of possession. The strategies are delightfully various but possession is paramount.

48. Ibid., p. 62.

49. René Girard, *Deceit Desire and the Novel* (Baltimore, 1965), p. 12. To facilitate application of the quote to *The Bostonians* I have feminized and italicized some of Girard's pronouns.

50. Henry Pelling, *American Labor* (Chicago, 1965), p. 61.

51. Employee pressure did exist, though it is difficult to date its emergence. Susan Porter Benson notes, 'In many early stores, the contrast between the luxurious public areas of the store and the behind-the-scenes areas reserved for the use of the employees was dramatic.' See her 'Palace of Consumption and Machine for Selling', *Radical History Review*, No. 21 (Fall 1979), 207–8.

52. *The Letters of Henry James*, Vol. 1 (London, 1920), p. 101

# Notes on Contributors

IAN BELL teaches literature in the Department of American Studies at the University of Keele. He is the author of *Critic as Scientist: The Modernist Poetics of Ezra Pound* (1981) and various essays on the intellectual resources of modernist aesthetics. He has previously edited *Ezra Pound: Tactics for Reading* (1982) in the Critical Studies series.

MILLICENT BELL teaches English and American literature at the University of Boston. She has published widely and substantially over virtually the whole range of nineteenth-century American fiction.

NICOLA BRADBURY is a lecturer in English at the University of Reading and is the author of *Henry James: The Later Novels* (1979).

ELLMAN CRASNOW read architecture at Cape Town and English at Cambridge and Yale; he is now a lecturer in the School of English and American Studies at the University of East Anglia. He has published on aspects of seventeenth-, nineteenth- and twentieth-century American writing, and is at present working on the poetry of John Ashberry. His paper in the present volume was originally delivered to the E.A.A.S. in Paris in 1982.

STUART CULVER teaches English and American literature at the University of Arkansas, Fayetteville. His work on Henry James has previously appeared in *E.L.H.* He has also written on contemporary critical theory and is currently involved in a study of James's rôle in the development of the literary profession.

MAUD ELLMANN is a lecturer in English at the University of Southampton. She is a co-editor of the *Oxford Literary Review* and the author of various essays on modernist texts. Her monograph on *The Politics of the Personality: Modernist Writing and the Question of the Subject* is to be published shortly.

RICHARD GODDEN teaches literature in the Department of American Studies at the University of Keele. He has published extensively on American writing of the '20s and '30s, and is currently working on narrative responses to late capitalism.

DAVID HOWARD is a Senior Lecturer in the Department of English and Related Literature at the University of York. He has previously published essays on Cooper, Hawthorne, James, Meredith and Stevens, and is at present writing a study of nineteenth-century American fiction.

# Index

187

# Index